MURAD OF SEPASTIA

"I just cannot recall any of our revolutionary fighters that has left such a deep and total impression on me as Murad of Sepastia. At this moment, even as I am writing these lines, Murad is before my eyes, with his bronzed, firm build and his deep, restless and fiery eyes, with his thick, shaggy eyebrows and an amazing head mounted erect on his masculine torso, displaying total power and certainty. His full and jet-black hair that started at mid-forehead and stood high, and looked like a bush, gave him the appearance of a lion. His forearms were muscular. He enjoyed restraining the wildest of horses. No one could ride and control the horse that he rode. He walked with a firm and energetic step; it seemed the earth shook as he strode."

—*Avetis Aharonian*
President of the Parliament of Armenia 1919

"So many Murads, and yet there is one whose masculine figure appears dominant, like one for whom Dante d'Aligeri might say: *Mai non pens ammo forma piu nobile d'Eroe.* We have never pictured a more noble hero."

—*Mikayel Varandian*

"Armenians have now lost all hope in diplomacy that has been deceitful; and in truth, for the Armenian people, there remains only to rely on its own moral forces, and to die, forsaking the so-called enlightened age that has shame and reproach engraved on its forehead … O, Armenian people, Europe has no pity. It is more bloodthirsty than our adversary of centuries. Do not even believe in it. It seeks its gains in blood and in the sacrifice of our innocent victims. Our hope must lie only in ourselves."

—*Hrair-Dzhokhk*
(Armenak Ghazarian)

MURAD
OF SEPASTIA

BY
MIKAYEL VARANDIAN

Translated and Edited with an Introduction
by Ara Ghazarians

ARMENIAN CULTURAL FOUNDATION
ARLINGTON, MASSACHUSETTS
2006

*This book was published through the generosity
of Anne and Mesrob Bchakjian.
The Armenian Cultural Foundation
expresses its gratitude.*

———◆———

MURAD OF SEPASTIA
By Mikayel Varandian

Published in 2006 by
Armenian Cultural Foundation
441 Mystic Street, Arlington, MA 02474

Originally published in Armenian as *Murad: Life and Work of a Warrior from Sepastia*,
by Hayrenik Press, Boston, 1931.

First published in English by Armenian Cultural Foundation, 2006.

Translated and Edited with an Introduction
by Ara Ghazarians

Cover & Book Design by
Arrow Graphics, Inc., Watertown, Massachusetts
info@arrow1.com
Printed in the United States of America

ISBN 13: 978-0-9674621-6-5
ISBN 10: 0-9674621-6-9
Library of Congress Control Number: 2006925649

*It is our responsibility to make sure we preserve
and document our history in order to
empower future generations*

Mesrob Bchakjian

*Anne Bchakjian, Hunter College Graduate and Educator for 38 years
Mesrob Maurice Bchakjian, Photoengraver, Lithographer,
Race Horse Owner and Breeder*

To the Memory of

The Bchakjian family members who were lost to
history during the Genocide of the Armenians at the
hands of the Turks in the desert of Der el Zor in 1915.

The Bouchakjian Family of Sepastia, 1914

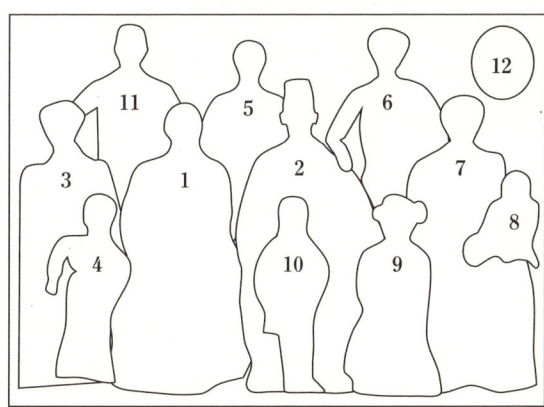

1 Grandmother,
   Mariam Bouchakjian
   Martyred 1915

2 Grandfather,
   Mesrob Bouchakjian
   Martyred 1915

3 Aunt Armenouhie
   Remarried (Margosian)

4 Cousin, Daughter of Armenouhie
   Name lost to history
   Martyred 1915

5 Father, Kerop Bouchakjian

6 Aunt Makrouhie
   Remarried (Ashjian)

7 Aunt Parendzem
   Martyred 1915

8 Cousin, Son of Parendzem
   Name Sumpat
   Martyred 1915

9 Cousin, Daughter of Parendzem
   Name lost to history
   Martyred 1915

10 Cousin Orjienne
    Son of Armenouhie
    Martyred 1915

11 Second cousin Ohaness
    Martyred 1915

12 An Uncle, Serop Mesrobian
    (Bouchakjian) immigrated to
    the USA in 1912

Of the pictured family members, the only survivors were Armenouhie, Makrouhie, and Kerop. They survived Der-Zor, reached Aleppo and eventually reached Marseille, France. ultimately arriving in the USA.

Three husbands of aunts pictured, and not in picture, were also martyred.

*Shoushan Hagopian, Murad's niece,
with Anne and Mesrob Bchakjian*

CONTENTS

Acknowledgements

Several people rendered their assistance in the realization of this project. I would like to express my deepest gratitude to Peter Najarian for his skilful copy-editing of this work, Armand Derian for his help in deciphering the Turkish phrases and their orthographical details, and Shushan Avagyan for her translation into English of Daniel Varuzhan's poem.

Introduction

During the first two decades of the twentieth century, the Armenian people experienced the most traumatic event in their millennia old history: the first major genocide of the twentieth century perpetrated by the government of Ottoman Turkey. An ancient civilization came to the brink of extinction. In contrast to this tragic picture were manifestations of true courage by thousands of selfless individual and collective acts of Herculean proportions. Although volumes have been written about the horrors of the Armenian Genocide, yet little has been said about thousands of unsung Armenian men and women who sacrificed their lives in the name of freedom, their fatherland, and the honor and dignity of their people.

This biography by Mikayel Varandian is a tribute to one unsung hero—one of the legendary figures of the twentieth century Armenian liberation movement, Murad Khrimian,[1] better known as Murad of Sepastia. Ranking with the elite members of the movement of the time, and like many of his compatriots, Murad was thrusted in the torrents of the revolutions, revolts, and battles of World War I to defend the Armenian people. This narrative traces Murad's life from his humble beginnings in his birthplace, Kovtun,[2] to his youth in Constantinople with anecdotal references to the events and his encounters with several Armenian and Turkish personalities of the time, among them General Andranik and Turkish figures such as Enver Pasha.

Varandian, a writer and intellectual, himself a prominent figure on a different sphere—sketches the revolutionary career of Murad from his hometown and district of Sepastia, where he immersed himself in educating youth and organizing the self-defense units among the peasantry to his great work in Armenia, Russia, Iran, and finally the Caucasus. He died on August 4, 1918, defending a strategic position in the sandy hilltops of the oil rich city of Baku, in a battle that was to shape the course of history in the Caucasus. His end thus came hundreds of miles from his native home in defense of his supreme ideals and nation, leaving behind a rich legacy.

Little is known about the origins of Murad's family. Born Murad, baptismal name Tonik, Tonakan[3] Hagopian, better known as Khrimian, the origins of this legendary figure's family are scanty and often contradictory. Some researchers have also disputed the date of Murad's birth. One source[4] lists the date of Murad's birth as 1872, another[5] 1874. One of the six[6] children of Tsaghik and Hakob Hakobian, a sieve worker, Murad grew up in Kovtun, where later he and his brothers built their own house.[7]

Marrying Agapi, a woman of strong character in her own right, they had one son, named Gevorg Chavush in memory of another legendary revolutionary figure. The horrors of the genocide, killings, uprooting and deportations also ruined Murad's family like thousands around them. Engulfed in revolutionary operations, Murad also got separated from his wife and son never to see them again. To this date, nothing is known of Agapi's fate, but their son Gevorg, upon reaching the Caucasus in the caravans of the survivors was adopted by an Armenian family who gave him a new surname and identity, Hayk Mshetsian. He grew up and lived in Soviet Armenia where he had married and had two children.[8]

As the Stalinist horrors began to hover over the Soviet republics, persecutions and purges also reached Armenia causing havoc in an already emaciated nation. Like hundreds and thousands of Soviet citizens, Hayk was also conscripted in the army to fight for "Mother Russia." He fought in the Red Army on the European theater of the War, where he was captured. Sensing the dark fate awaiting the returning Red Army POWs who were to be persecuted on the fictitious charges of espionage, Hayk, along with a large contingent of the Red Army Armenian soldiers, defected to the West carrying with him the guilt of leaving his family behind in Yerevan. In 1945, now under a new identity Hayk Khachaturian immigrated to the United States[9] and settled in Philadelphia,[10] where he died in 1975.

The author of this biography, Mikayel Varandian [né Mikayel Hovhannisian], was an exceptional figure on his own rights. An intellectual, philosopher, political theorist and activist, writer, editor, and diplomat, born in Shushi, the cultural citadel of Karabakh in 1874, Varandian received his early education in his birthplace. Upon graduating from high school in the early 1880s, he left for Geneva to receive his higher education, where he became one of the active members of the Armenian student groups. Concurrent with his academic studies, he joined the founding members of the periodical *Droshak* [Flag] the official organ of the Armenian Revolutionary Federation (ARF). In addition to his academic engagements, Varandian began contributing to several major Armenian periodicals such as *Murch* [Hammer], and *Mshak* [Laborer] with the *nom de plume* Eko. Upon graduation in 1897, Varandian moved to Bulgaria and Romania and immersed himself in political activities. In 1898, he assumed the interim editorship of *Droshak*, where he worked intermittently until the outbreak of World War I, contributing numerous editorials, articles, op eds, studies, and biographies. Most of his works later were compiled and appeared in his two major volumes *Haykakan sharzhman nakhapatmut'iwně* (The Pre-History of the Armenian Movement), and *Hosank'ner* (Currents). After the first Russian Revolution in 1905, he moved to the Caucasus, joining the editorial board of *Haraj* (Forward) and other papers. It was during this period that he wrote his *Kovkasean Vandea* (The Caucasian Vendetta), and many other articles. In 1907 Varandian left for Vienna, and then to Geneva where he assumed the editorship of *Droshak*.

Varandian also served on the Armenian National Delegation under Poghos Nubar Pasha until the establishment of the Republic of Armenia, when he was appointed Ambassador to Rome. The collapse of the Armenian Republic, the Treaty of Lausanne, and the eventual loss of Armenia's independence and freedom deeply depressed Varandian. Leaving public life, Varandian continued his literary activities publishing his the first volume of his *H. H. Dashnaktst'ean Patmut'iwn* (History of the A. R. Federation). The second volume of this history as well as two biographies one of *Murad of Sepastia* and the other of *Simon Zawarian*, were published posthumously. Varandian died in Paris in 1934.

Murad of Sepastia is the most comprehensive piece on the life and legacy of Murad of Sepastia. The first Armenian edition, published in 1931, was sponsored by the Central Executive of the Murad Fund.[11] With the exception of a number of short articles and essays,[12] surprisingly no other extensive works have been dedicated to his life. Interestingly, Murad kept a diary,[13] though very short (January 1- November 29, 1915) which is a true and modest portrayal of his life and activities.

Varandian's study is replete with hundreds of persons and place names, and *nom de guerres* of Armenian freedom fighters, and revolutionaries. Deeply involved in the political and revolutionary activities of his time and having served on the editorial boards of several party papers, Varandian knew many of these figures. Readers interested in the legacy of these men and women are advised to consult available documentary, reference and source materials.[14] For the purposes of this work, only brief biographical information on the most prominent and central figures, such as General Andranik, and Sepuh is provided. All the annotations other than those identified by *(V)* for Varandian are those of the translator. The Library of Congress transliteration key with some modifications has been consulted. The preamble titled "The Book of Heroes" by Varandian follows this introduction.

A word on works like *Murad of Sepastia* in the Soviet period and since. The Bolsheviks buried the names and memories of hundreds of national heroes such as Murad, considering them reactionaries and pro-imperialist enemies of socialism. However, with the collapse of the Soviet Union and the birth of an independent Armenia in 1991, a true history of the early twentieth century is being rewritten. Names once banished are reclaimed and rehabilitated; hidden or forgotten memoirs and diaries are being rediscovered and published;[15] archival resources are opened to the public; and memoirs and analytical works by historians of major figures are being published.[16]

As a result of this activity, the young generation in Armenia is learning about these figures who sacrificed all to save their nation; and this knowledge is an indispensable part of the republic's educational agenda. In the words of a prominent Armenian scholar, "Not a single nation can make its future without properly examining its past. The First Republic of

Armenia gives us a number of dedicated national leaders who were ready to sacrifice their lives to sustain our first state."[17]

The publication of this work represents an important contribution to that effort. It owes its existence to the inspiration and generosity of the family of Mesrob Bchakjian, many of whose ancestors from Sepastia perished during the Armenian Genocide of World War I. As Mesrob Bchakjian has stated, the purpose of this volume is "to inform the English-speaking Armenians in the dispersion of their history and in the hopes of nurturing their precious heritage." We thank Mr. Bchakjian, and it is our hope that this inaugural work on Murad of Sepastia will inspire others to sponsor similar projects to strengthen the sense of national identity and imbue our English-speaking young generation with pride in and knowledge of their ancestral heritage.

Ara Ghazarians
Boston, 2006

Notes

[1] Murad's family name is Hakobian. However, he and his family have been known as the Khrimians [of Crimea], which is attributed to two things: one to the origins of his ancestors who are known to have settled in Sepastia from Crimea, and the second to Catholicos Mkrtich Khrimian, whose last name is Murad to have adopted out of immense respect for that venerable clergy and historic figure.

[2] Kovtun (Cow House in Armenian), once an entirely Armenian village still exists in Turkey, though cleared of its Armenian residents, and renamed Göydün.

[3] The name was given to Murad by his parents in the memory of his maternal uncle. Source: Oral History narrative with Murad's sister, Mariam Hagopian-Elmasian.

[4] Vahan Hambardzumian, *Village World* [Giwghashkharh]: *An Historical Cultural Study of Govdoon*. Providence, RI, 2001.

[5] Antranig Ch'alapian, *Heghap'okhakan demk'er* (Revolutionary Figures). Michigan, 1991.

[6] Two sisters, Serbuhi and Mariam, and three brothers Hovhannes, Tigran, and Karapet.

[7] To this day the site of the Murad's house is remembered by the local elders of Kovtun as attested by a group of Armenian tourists who traveled to Kovtun in 1993.

[8] Hayk Mshetsian married one Siranush Tosunian and they had two daughters Azniv and Lena, who at present live in Moscow and Yerevan, respectively. Both are married and live with their children and grandchildren.

[9] The American National Committee for Homeless Armenians (ANCHA), formed in 1945 through the efforts of George Mardikian, Armenian food consultant and restaurateur, a native of Babert, Western Armenia, himself an orphan of the Armenian Genocide, calling on the Displaced Persons Act of the U.S. Congress, succeeded in aiding 25,000 Armenians' immigration to the United States.

[10] As his new life began to take roots in his adopted homeland, Hayk expressed his interest in joining the ranks of the A.R.F. His application was turned down as the party suspected of his true identity despite the fact that his aunt, Mariam Hagopian, Murad's sister, had vouched for his identity. Source: interview with Mrs. Shushan Hagopian, Murad's niece of Springfield, Massachusetts.

[11] The Murad Fund was established shortly after the death of the Murad of Sepastia in his memory in Providence, Rhode Island by his compatriots. Articles 1 and 3 of its By-Laws read: "The goal of the Murad Fund is to establish a Higher Academic Institution in the name and unwading memory of Murad . . . to materialize that object, the Fund has to raise $25,000 dollars." The dream never materialized.

[12] Consult the bibliography provided in this book.

[13] Murad's diary was published in three-part series in the Journal *Vem*. The original version of the handwritten diary is kept at the Armenian General Benevolent Union (A.G.B.U.) Nubarian Repository in Paris, France. His close comrade-in-arms, Egho of Zmar, also kept a diary the whereabouts of which is unknown. Murad's diary served as a primary source material for the famous Armenian writer and journalist Zapel Esayian, who used in her writing of *Muradi odisakanĕ Svazen Bat'um* (Murad's Odyssey from Sivas to Batum).

[14] Awo. *Heghap'okhakan Alpom: Azatagrakan Payk'ari Hushamatean* (Revolutionary Album: Liberation Struggle Memorial Book). Halep, 1981.

[15] Some of the works known to us include, A. Ch'alapian, *Zoravar Andranik ew hay heghap'okhakan sharzhumĕ* (General Andranik and the Armenian Revolutionary Movement). Southfield, Michigan, 1984. Hamlet Gevorgyan, *Dro: kensagrakan, husher, vkayut'yunner* (Dro: Biography, Memories, Testimonials). Erevan, 1991. Hamlet Gevorgyan, *Dro*. Erevan, 1999. A. Nersisyan, *Avetik Sahakyan, [Hayr Abraham]*. Erevan, 2003. A. Ch'alapian, *Dro: (Drastamat Kanayan)*. Michigan, 2003. A. Nersisyan, *Zoravar Sepuh. Aprogh herosner matenashar, t'iv 3* (General Sepuh: Living Heroes Series #3). Erevan, 2005.

[16] James G. Mandalian, *Armenian Freedom Fighters: The Memoirs of Rouben Der Minasian*. Boston, 1963. Simon Vratzian, *Tempest-born Dro*. New York, 2000.

[17] Babken Harutyunyan, in "Appreciation of National Heroes Emerges as Daily Necessity," by Karine Mangassaryan..

The Book of Heroes

The heart-warming song of the golden canary has become the immortal symbol for coming of the Vardans in the Battle of Avarayr.[1] How many such battles have there been in the history of Armenians, and yet our freedom fighters still await their Eliseus. Let us at least write of them.

Jean Jacque Rousseau once said in his *Confessions* that anyone's biography would be quite a book if written with complete sincerity and frankness. So may we write about the heroes of the Armenian liberation movement and their turbulent lives, despite how they may have wanted out of modesty to remain in the shadows of history. Among them only Andranik has left a memoir, which is now in the *Droshak* archives, but this too is incomplete.

Where are Kristapor's and Simon's and Rostom's?

Where are Serop's, Eprem's, Duman's, Keri's, Aram's, Hrair's, Chavush's, and Murads? Ishkhan's, Hamazasp's, Sako's, Khecho's, Apro's, and Gurgen's? Avo of Trebizond, Maloyan of Gumri, Nikol of Karabagh, Vardapet Vardan, Kaytsak [Thunder] Arakel, Makar of Spaghan, Ishkhan of Van, Kosti, Vazgen Teroyian, Hovsep Arghutian, Aram Aramian, Babken Siwni, Gnuni, Khan, and Kukunian?[2]

Mikayel Varandian

Where are the memoirs of Turbakh, Sargis, Vahan, Ashot-Erkat [the Iron], Aristakes Zorian, and Galust Aloyian? Where are the books of our late intellectuals, Aknuni, Vramian, Honan, Zavrian and Zargarian, Garo and Hrach, Khazhak and Shahrik, Siamanto and Varuzhan, Sargis Minasian, Shahbaz and Sevak, Galfayian and Topchian, Mateos and Pilos, Bardogh and Babken and hundreds of others?

Where are the books of our old revolutionaries be they Dashnak, Hunchak or Armenakan: Arabo, Levon, Huno, Kara Melik, Achekgeozian, Chato and Shero, Murat Poyajian, Jirair, Peto, Yusufian, Keri of Dersim, Avetisian, Shmavon, Barsegh Zakarian, and Manuk Shatvorian?

And the list goes on and on. No, the dead did not wish to write of their stormy lives. Alas, it is left to us to write of them, despite having to rely on documents and notes, we who are more fortunate in having escaped the horrors of our history, we who have a kind of moral debt to our deceased, who themselves are so worthy of our gratitude. There are thousands of them who sacrificed their lives for their compatriots, so many who have vanished unburied in unknown trenches. Their graves are our hearts.

Their deeds must be recorded so that our memory of them will live from generation to generation. The stories of their lives must be told.

Perhaps one day we should also declare a day of heroes and celebrate them nationally, the same way we have adopted April 24 as a day for our martyrs.[3]

We do not have a pantheon or a national cathedral where we could inter their remains and honor their bravery like most civilized nations. We do not have a tomb of the "Unknown Soldier," before which we could kneel and mourn in gratitude.

We can only offer our collective honor by pen and speech in biographies and public gatherings.

This is a kind of sacred debt, and it rests on the shoulders of all us diaspora Armenians.

And this includes you, our young and our intellectuals, dispersed throughout the world even in its remote corners. You who have the skill of writing and who live with the memory of a homeland, who become excited by the tales of these legendary heroes and who would like to live with equal selflessness and even moments of supreme passion. It is you who have to wipe the moss from those blessed graves that have been so dishonored. It is you who should bring them out from the depths of dark oblivion and display them with shining images.

Gather with compassion the remains of our heroes, their letters and photographs and documents and memorabilia, along with the memories of our elders who knew them. Write of them and create a vibrant literature of our glorious Armenian history.

Even primitive tribes worship their *igits*,[4] and bestow this worship to following generations by word of mouth.

Are we any less in our devotion?

Our heroes will pass and disappear in the mist of time. Let us try to keep their spirit alive. They are our honor, our glory and our pride. They are the masthead of our honorable and civilized race. They are our spiritual treasure, without which we would be insignificant remnants of history, like dust in the winds. Let us carry out our duty to our dead if we do not want history to put its black seal on our forehead. Let us etch in the consciousness of our future generations their idealism; let us immortalize them like those in a legendary Hellenic epic. Saluting heroes is one of one of the most important acts of civilization, and one that can advance it even further.

* * *

And now to Murad.

The Armenian liberation movement has had several Murads in its history. There are also many Nikols, Khechos, and Ashots, and so on. However, there is always one who occupies a special place in our hearts for his exceptional gallantry.

We have heard of Nikol, or Duman-Nikol, one of the earliest military and intellectual leaders of the movement, who in 1914, devastated by a ruthless calamity and unable to participate in the battle against the enemy, chose to put an end to his turbulent life with a pistol.

We have heard of Khecho, that modest giant whose bravery and selflessness matched his titanic figure. Dashnak Khecho who in 1915 in the vicinity of Datvan fell to his death in a bloody and fierce battle, leaving a deep sigh in the ranks and file.

Then there was Aram Aramian, that tall and handsome figure, who in 1899 in Erzurum shouted of Revolution and Liberty in the faces of his Turkish executioners as he stood on the gallows.

Nor will we forget Murad of Tsronk and old Murad Poyachian, both of whom were part of the revolts in Sasun in 1890s, the former rotting in Turkish prisons in the last twelve years of his life and then martyred in 1915.

So many Murads, and yet there is one whose masculine figure appears dominant, like one for whom Dante d'Aligeri might say:

"Mai non pens ammo forma piu nobile d'Eroe. — We have never pictured a more noble hero."

This is Murad of Sepastia, in whose glorious memory we dedicate this modest work.

We are helped by the memoirs of his inseparable comrade, the prominent Sepuh, and the also inseparable though wandering Vardan Shahbaz, as well as the renown activist Tasnapetian from Jerusalem, the intellectual Vahan Hambardzumian who was from his same village, Levon Mesrop from Marseille who knew him since 1895 in Constantinople, Mikayelian who had accompanied him during his tragic 1915 odyssey from Sepastia to Batum, Archbishop Nerses Melik-Tangian who was his comrade in 1905-1906 in Zangezur, and Reverend Father Mesrop Eranosian, Tigran Devoian, Harutiun Tellalian, and Oskan Erkanian who provided us with more fascinating details about his life and deeds.

And finally, Murad's sister, whom we had the opportunity to interview at length in the suburb of St. Antoine near Marseille,[5] where she had settled in recent years with her husband and children.

We thank them all.

We also want to express our deep gratitude to the Sepastia Compatriot Society of America and its Murad Fund, whose generous sponsorship has helped us realize this project and whose members are imbued with the deepest love for their native son. This biography is one of the first of their projects to honor him.

Despite being unprepared for such a task, I did not wish to turn down their request, since I too have had enthusiasm for the warrior that goes back to when in 1905, along with his comrades in the Caucasus, he repulsed the Tatars with fierce attacks. One of those comrades, a serious though uneducated man, also contributed to our endeavor with his fierce debates in our meetings in Tbilisi.

Mikayel Varandian
Paris, 1930

Notes

[1] Epic battle fought in the plain of Avarayr, at present in the vicinity of the city of Khoy in the Western Azerbaijan province of Iran, where in 451 A.D. Armenians fought against the Sasanid Persia to uphold their Christian faith. Overwhelmed and defeated by the Persian armies, the outcome of the battle is considered a moral victory in the history of the Armenian people as they succeeded in keeping their faith.

[2] The names of the three founders of the Armenian Revolutionary Federation, followed by a list of freedom fighters, revolutionary leaders and commanders.

[3] The reference is to April 24, 1915 when the Turkish government rounded up hundreds of Armenian community leaders and intellectuals in Constantinople and various districts throughout the Ottoman Empire, marking the beginning of the Armenian Genocide (1915-1923). This symbolic day has been adopted by the Armenians throughout the world in commemoration of the 1.5 million Armenians, who perished, and another estimated 600,000 who were exiled from their ancestral homeland and dispatched to the Arabian deserts.

[4] *Igit*, brave.

[5] See Murad's sister Mariam Hakobian-Elmasian's family picture on page 125.

I

Childhood and Youth

All that we know about Murad's early years is provided by an unpublished memoir of Sepuh, whom Murad himself trusted.

The warrior was born in the village of Kovtun,[1] Sepastia,[2] in 1874, in a family of refugees who bore the last name Khrimian and who supposedly had settled in Kovtun in the early 1870s.

From where they migrated is unknown, however we do know that there was no connection between Murad's family and Khrimian Hayrik.[3] The general belief is that the Khrimian family had Romany origins.

One of our young comrades, Vahan Hambardzumian, who is also from Kovtun, has argued that the fact of being a Romany was sufficient grounds for discrimination, since the people there did not view the Romanies favorably.

Sepuh[4] also added that Murad's Armenian antagonists would try to insult and offend him by referring to him as a "child of a Romany."

Nevertheless, this was not the first time that one of non-Armenian blood would be assimilated into the Armenian homeland and be nurtured by its language and culture so

I

Sepuh

completely that he would become such a staunch patriot. Let us recall the Papazians, who have given us a prominent Armenian writer and a revolutionary, and also in the Middle Ages the number of leaders and warriors among whom the greatest was Vardan Mamikonian.[5]

* * *

The family of Murad Hakobian-Khrimian was an adventurous clan whose ancestors had been valiant fighters, thus the young Murad was nurtured in its traditions and in particular was often told about the bravery of his grandfather Sargis. So too would he himself someday tell his own stories in his plain and rustic, but graceful and colorful dialect.

Where was the patriarch Sargis from? Murad himself did not know but would say only that he probably had emigrated from Khrim, Crimea, and because of this, his family was called Khrimian.

Sieve-maker by trade, Sargis had traveled extensively and seen many lands, always living under a tent, his only companion a mule. He was a free-spirited and carefree child of nature who wandered everywhere, often for no other reason but the passion of wandering itself, sometimes in the plains or in the valleys on the banks of bubbling springs. He felt himself at home everywhere. He was fearless and had no foes, both mountain bandits and prosperous villagers were his friends, and since a sieve-maker was always welcomed he visited many homes.

He was even a fortune-teller. He knew how to read in cards the mist of the future and encourage the destitute with rosy predictions and excite lovers to reach for their dreams.

Grandfather Sargis was a proud man who was deeply sensitive to his family's honor and integrity. God forbid if anyone dared to desecrate or insult it, for like an injured person who nurtures revenge in silence and waits for an opportune moment, he would strike his fatal blow and then disappear like a demon.

There was not a place Sargis had not been. He had traveled throughout the Crimea several times. He had criss-crossed the vast steppes of Russia. He had been to the Caucasus and journeyed through the mountains of Daghestan.[6] He had toured in Turkish Armenia the cities of Erzurum, Van, and Mush, and after he had been to the depths of Arabia, he brought with him on his return two beautiful stallions.

Back in Crimea, he finally wanted to retire, but an unexpected incident made him renew his adventurous travels. For a long time a Tatar[7] had his eyes on Sargis' beautiful wife, and one night he dared to enter Sargis' tent and violate her. Sargis killed him on the spot, and then, to avoid an investigation and prosecution, he took his wife and children away once again and left for abroad. This time he went to the cities of Karin,[8] Erzincan,[9] and Kemakh[10] in Turkish Armenia, continuing to wander until a very advanced age, always in pursuit of new adventures. After clashes with Turkish authorities and the killing a few janissaries, death finally put an end to his turbulent life.

The baby Murad was nurtured with such stories as that of Sargis, and they enriched his sharp mind and rich imagination.

Sargis' children, however, both Hakob and Mkr, or Mkrtich, had severed themselves from their ancestral tradition of wandering, and they had settled in Kovtun. Hakob had four children; one of them would be our future hero.

Some Armenians in Kovtun were against gypsies settling in their village. The stormy past and bloody adventures of their marauding forefathers terrified the Armenian peasants, and the village was split into two camps. However, the supporters of Hakob, having more clout, emerged victorious.

* * *

The village of Kovtun, which was mostly Armenian was located on the east of Sepastia, on the banks of the Alis River, and it had about three hundred households. A little farther from the river on the top of a hill were the pastures called Palekhlu, where day in day out grazed their famous horses. A little farther were the impassable swamps. Then to the north rose the Sakhar Mountains that soared to the sky with summer pastures for sheep and cattle.

One of the mountains, Siuri, was the summer resort for the villagers. In the east and northeast lay the vast farmlands.

Kovtun also had its pilgrimage sites. The most prominent was St. Karapet,[11] where during Vardavar[12] and other feasts the surrounding villages assembled to pray and offer their

4

Kovtun in 1978

sacrifices, dancing and feasting and celebrating with wrestling matches and so forth. The people of Sepastia loved wrestling and there was not anyone from there who was not trained in it.

St. Karapet was a rendezvous for Armenian Christians, and during the years of drought men and women from the nearby villages, both young and old, would come to seek the blessings of the reverend fathers and beg for rain for the parched earth.

Since Murad had not received any education, he was almost illiterate, like Andranik[13] and many others of our fighters. Yet he was endowed with many skills that he would use not only in the battlefield but also in party meetings with more educated youth during hot debates.

In those days the only educated ones in Armenian villages were the priests, like Fr. Todik.

When he was barely eight years old, Murad was sent to Fr. Todik's school, but he couldn't stand its disciplinary regime and didn't stay. The sensitive soul of our hero revolted against

5

the head-teacher who was called a caliph and who was ruthless with the innocent children.

"If my strength had allowed it," Murad would say later, "I would have skewered that caliph on the spot."

He left the school and became a shepherd for a farmer.

The young Murad is portrayed as a modest and noble boy compassionate toward the weak and ruthless with their oppressors. He was also eloquent and smart and loved by his friends.

Once, he himself talked about his rebellion against oppression.

"In the village" he said, "there were a few rich kids who always looked down on me and my friends. Whenever we took our cattle to the pasture they would not allow us to proceed so we had to change our path and take another one. Every time I told my father and elder brothers about them they would advise me to be accommodating because we were dealing with the children of the wealthy. And so days went by while the rich kids continued their behavior as if they were devoted to it.

"There is a limit to everything, including patience. The behavior of the *aghas*[14] had become unbearable, and after a lot of thinking I decided to organize my friends and teach those arrogant kids a lesson. One morning when we led our herd toward St. Karapet, my friends all swore to carry out my orders if a fight broke out. Anyone who broke this vow would be expelled and punished as a traitor." "One for all and all for one." we said, "We have to fight until those rich kids treat us fairly."

"After we took our oath we were approached as usual, and I dispatched some of us to tell them our cattle were going to graze in the pasture and we were not going to allow anyone else to bring his cattle there.

6

"The rich kids disregarded the message and attempted to assault the messengers, but at that moment my buddies and I made a surprise attack and they fled. When they returned we beat them up again."

This incident caused quite a commotion. Some wanted to avenge Murad and his comrades, but others intervened and the dispute was resolved. Thereafter Murad became the leader of his group and organized them and trained them in self-defense.

Later on, clashes also took place with the cattle herders from a neighboring Turkish village, but Murad and his comrades always emerged victorious.

One day on his way to Kovtun, a group of youths ambushed and blocked his passage and wanted to kill him, but armed with only a pocketknife he faced up to them bravely and made them all flee.

Hunting was one of his hobbies, and he often went to the shores of the Alis River and to the marshlands that were full of ducks and geese, secretly taking his uncle's rifle.

He was the strongest among his peers and the most skilled equestrian, as well as the best marksman. He had learned these skills from his uncle, who was famous for them.

He was also a skilled dancer during the celebrations of the pilgrimages, and as the star of the wrestlers he became the subject of feminine gossip and crushes. All the prizes and awards always went to him.

* * *

The Darbin[ian]s were the village's wealthiest family, and though Murad worked for them he never dared to lay an eye on their beautiful daughter. However she would dance around him like a butterfly, and away from her mother's eyes she would save him the best of the kitchen in a bag.

He too was in love with her, but not daring to exchange a word each of them felt suffocated by the puritanical customs of their patriarchal families.

Then came the feasts of Vardavar when everyone filled his cart and mounted his horse and headed for the Monastery of Hreshtakapet,[15] including Murad who headed a large contingent of boys with joyful laughter, then both young and old sat on the ground enjoying the kebab and wine. And on that night of Lusnkay[16] when bonfires crackled under a starlit sky everywhere was filled with song and dance in an air most fit for lovers.

Here too had come the Darbins, and the two lovers sought each other, the young lad searching while the lass sat waiting.

From tent to tent and carriage to carriage he searched until he found her a short distance from her parent's tent. He had decided to divulge his feelings to her. He knew that her family would not consent, and he had decided to kidnap her and fly from mountain to valley like a hawk heedless of any obstacle.

Passing her he whispered to her ear:

"I will see you tomorrow near the Lusaghbiwr spring and we will talk."

"I will be there," she responded.

The Lusaghbiwr was located south of the Monastery of Hreshtakapet, and the rendezvous was to be during the feasts.

When the hour arrived he waited impatiently but she was late. Her parents' supervision was very strict, but she eventually showed up and they opened their hearts to each other, the girl accepting her lover's proposition to run away.

"I cannot be worthy of your love any other way," he said. "The differences between you and me are enormous. You are rich, and I poor. It leaves me no other choice but to get you by force. I will prepare the horses and when the time comes we will disappear and seek our hearth in a humble home."

But as the young man was reviewing their escape plan, an unanticipated incident turned everything upside down.

Since his childhood days he had many enemies, both Armenian and Turkish. On that day when a group of Turks blocked his way wanting to kill him, he had struck one of them before they fled. The news had spread fast to Sepastia and with the police now coming to arrest him he vanished into the mountains of Sakhar. Then after his parents said they knew nothing of the incident, the police arrested Hakob, Murad's father, so Murad, learning the news of his father's arrest, immediately returned from the mountains and surrendered to them for his father's release. A few months later Murad was also released for being a juvenile.

However he could no longer stay in the village, so he bade farewell to his ancestral hearth, buried his first love in his heart, and left for Constantinople where he endured sad days as a laborer and a porter.

II

The Assassin

Le piongnard, seul espoir de la terre
Es ton arme sacre.[17]

André Chenier

It was 1890 when Murad, turning seventeen, arrived in the Ottoman capital. This was a prominent year in the lives of Armenians. Revolutionary movements were sprouting throughout the country. There was a rebellion in Erzurum and a Gum-Gapu[18] demonstration in Constantinople. When the Armenian newspapers and magazines picked up the news there were meetings in the National Assembly in regard to the Armenian Question. All this fired Murad's passions and stirred a deep patriotism in the young porter's psyche.

He became acquainted with a young Armenian named Lusinian, who suggested he attend a Sunday school, which had just been opened at a hall adjacent to St. Lusavorich Church of the Galatia neighborhood, and he began attending enthusiastically. Then after learning the alphabet he was able to read in just a few months, and he began devouring the news in the papers.

Through Lusinian, he joined several Armenian organizations and circles until he found the clandestine one of the Hunchaks,[19] and he carried out secret assignments with zeal and selflessness, delivering documents to dangerous places and transporting daggers and pistols.

According to our comrade Zatik, in 1893 the Armenian Patriarch [Khoren] Achegian, an obsequious yet autocratic person who was much disliked, publicly dishonored Armenian revolutionaries and called them *"stahak,"* scoundrels. Thereafter the Hunchak Party ordered all senior clergies in all neighborhoods not to mention his name during the service, and when they gathered at St. Lusavorich church in Galatia and refused to name him anxiety spread everywhere in Constantinople.

The police under the jurisdiction of the Patriarch closed the gates of the church courtyard that was filled with a large crowd, and when a compatriot who had come late was barred from entering he was beaten by the police for disregarding their orders and showing resistance. At that moment, Murad, who was in the crowd, opened the gate and clashed with the police and freed the man from their hands and brought him in.

Knowing the police were not going to bear such humiliation, and would return in a larger number to arrest Murad, the crowd immediately collected nine gold coins for him and asked him to leave through the back door, led by a Hunchak compatriot who would find him shelter.

The Armenian community at that time was filled with spies and traitors who must have known Murad was part of a secret committee, but they did not have the courage to approach him. On the other hand the Sultan's government, which had doubled its number of the spies, issued a strict order to arrest him.

This however would not be easy. When a squad of policemen and soldiers came to arrest him, the gallant lad with two pistols in his hands jumped to the street and ran toward the Galatia church and ordered its gates be closed, thus imprisoning himself and his terrified compatriots. When the police and the Turkish mob tried to smash the gates, Murad with pistols in hand threatened them to leave.

"*Teslim, teslim, giavoor*—surrender, surrender, infidel," the mob shouted, implying there would otherwise be bloodshed.

But the insurgent Murad replied that he would surrender only to a European ambassador.

When the outraged police tried to smash the gate, a shot came from above and one of them fell covered in blood, seriously wounded. Those blockading the church dispersed and by night the mob was gone, leaving only a handful of policemen to stand guard.

Murad in the meantime spent the night moving from one location to another with the help of supporters, and the night passed without an incident.

Early next morning a couple of people arrived from the Patriarchate to convince him to surrender, saying the Sultan would pardon him.

But the young man resolutely rejected this, saying "I do not believe any of the Sultan's promises," reiterating that he would surrender only to European legates.

Finally, at the request of Patriarch [Matt'eos III] Izmirlian, the ambassadors interceded, and with their guarantees Murad boarded a ship and left for Egypt.

* * *

One of the eyewitnesses of the young Sepastian's adventure, Levon Mesrop, a student at the Kendronakan [central] School at the time, reported the following in his memoirs.

"At that time Constantinople Armenians lived in an unprecedented period of commotion. Reform Programs,[20] the interest of the foreign governments with the Armenian Question, the support of the Patriarch Izmirlian, the amnesty of hundreds of the tortured political activists and prisoners from the remotest of colonies, had raised hope and enthusiasm.

"In the meantime the Kendronakan School was giving birth to a generation of 'Babgen Siwnis'.[21]

"One day, those who lived around the church noticed a young man from the provinces who was well-built and bright faced, but with sad eyes. There was something unusual about his warrior-like presence in a circle where informants and even the police had free access.

"His secret was soon revealed. He was a revolutionary who had eluded the police who had been following him for weeks, until he finally took refuge in the Galatia church.

"Interceding, the 'Iron Patriarch'[22] agreed to expel him from Constantinople on condition that he remain within the church courtyard until the conclusion of the negotiations

"The next day brought another surprise when the church and its surrounding buildings were encircled by police. Opposite the main gate several informants were napping on café stools when there appeared only a few steps away a young warrior wearing a red *papakh*[23] on his head bearing the silver logo of the Hunchak Party. He was Murad of Kovtun, the former night watchman of the Beaumonte beer factory of Shishli, and he would stay about a month in the church compound.

"The hall of the National Assembly, which had become useless after the National Constitution had been revoked, would soon become the meeting place of the boys in the Kendronakan School who were mesmerized by the Hunchak revolutionary and now surrounded him protectively.

"Though he was a plain and barely educated provincial worker who seemed taciturn and walked calmly with heavy steps, there was something in his character of a brave *fedayee*[24] warrior that was new to us, and he became the hero of our student body, the seniors in particular, who were mostly Dashnaks. However, this was at a time when the Dashnak Party[25] had not been solidified, and the young worshipped the idea of revolution regardless of any labels for it.

"I was the youngest of Kendronakan's student body and one of the smallest as well, which may have made me appear unique.

"Every evening a pack of informants would stop and search a group of students, upper classmen in particular, in one of the alleys near the school. After a number of the seniors were arrested and surveillance grew more intense, Murad appointed me as a messenger and then later his secretary.

"Workers from Mush, Sepastia, and Van would come to be enrolled as revolutionaries and register their pseudonyms, or *noms de guerre*, on a large sheet of paper, and their number would exceed two hundred. It was the responsibility of these new members to bear arms and abstain from alcohol, vodka in particular.

"One Sunday a group of fedayees appeared and one of them was drunk.

"'Why did you come?' Murad asked.

"To sign up as a Hunchak, he responded.

"'Come,' Murad said.

"He took the young man to the top of the stairs and sat him down and then turned to me and said, 'Plech, when you grow up, you should never drink vodka, it is not a drink worthy of a revolutionary, an alcoholic cannot become a revolutionary.'

"In the evenings about four of us from Kovtun would gather around him. The level of respect the others had for this young man astonished me, since they were all were older and seasoned revolutionaries.

"I remember a small anecdote that would turn into something serious.

"A few boys from the lower classes had been jailed for having associated with Murad. Every day Murad would approach the church gate and shower the informants and the policemen with a barrage of admonitions. One day I saw a boy from Mush, named Mushegh, a former Hunchak who had become an informant in the student body.

14

"In the evening, after the last block of classes, I went to the Assembly hall to receive Murad's orders as usual.

"'Sit,' Murad said, 'I have something to say.'

"Then after the visitors left he sent me to see if Kendron-akan 's students and staff had left. Both buildings of the school and the church were closed. The day's commotion had been replaced with a mystic silence as the sun set on the Galatia.

"Upon my return I found Murad alone, immersed in thoughts in the large hall. He paced up and down and wiped his forehead and hands with his large red handkerchief, a sign of his anger or agitation.

"'Go,' he said, 'and get a pitcher of wine and two meters of rope from Poghos,' a grocer from Sepastia on the church street. 'No one should see you bringing them here, not even the people of the winery, now, go.'

"I ran and told the grocer that the wine was for the classroom and the rope was to be used for the kindergarten games.

"Holding the large wine pitcher as low as I could I passed before a window and entered the assembly hall.

"Inside Murad was sitting at the head of the table with his red handkerchief in his hand. Shortly after appeared Mushegh the informant with his hands crossed, repeating imploringly: 'For God's sake, Murad, topa[26] Murad, let me leave, I will be back, let me leave.'

"'Plech,' Murad said to me, 'put the wine here with two cups and go home.'

"We went to the next room and he closed the door on the informant.

"'I need the rope,' he said.

"I gave it to him and fearfully asked him, 'What are you going to do with the rope?'

"'I am going to strangle this dog, so leave now.'

"I looked at him horrified, and then asked to stay.

"He agreed approvingly. I asked how he had captured Mushegh. He explained in a few words how he had seen him opposite the church gate and decided to teach a lesson to this monster, who should have been grateful for being enrolled in the Hunchak party.

"During the afternoon recess the policemen had withdrawn to the corners of the street blocks, assigning an Armenian informant to watch the large Gate. But Murad grabbed his former friend by the neck and forced him ahead. He had found a loaded pistol on him, a dagger, and some papers.

"When we returned to the hall Murad sat on his chair and poured the wine glasses.

"'Drink,' he said to the traitor. 'Drink now, my old Mushegh, my comrade Mushegh, who had taken an oath and became a revolutionary, drink, Hunchak Mushegh.'

"In the meantime he had given me an envelope of papers to examine. There were letters, dirty pieces of paper, and a notebook in which the names of everyone in the Kendronakan School including the faculty as well as some unfamiliar to me, each one numbered and annotated in Turkish but with Armenian script.

"Mushegh trembled and begged and cried but failed to escape the judgment.

"'For the love of this church, for the love of Christ, let your buddy go, Murad topa, let me go, let me go.'

"This scene lasted almost an hour, Murad silently and calmly watching the agony of the traitor. Finally he stood up and asking me to leave accompanied me to the door.

"At that point, mustering my courage, I said that with the killing of the Armenian informant the entire staff of the Kendronakan and the church would be endangered.

"Just then one of his friends from Kovtun walked in and learned of what was going on and convinced him to change his mind.

"We entered the room next door and Murad put the piece of rope on the table and turning to the traitor said: 'I would have strangled you with this and thrown your corpse from the window to the Turks.'

"Then unleashing his rage with curses he started disciplining the traitor who curled on the floor at his feet with his bloody face and torn clothes.

"'Pray for these guys who have kept me from killing you,' Murad said to him, 'take this bottle and get out of here, this bottle for which you betrayed us, you dog.'

"Then he made the spy take the wine and promise to leave Constantinople for good.

"A few days later we learned Mushegh had been killed in the vicinity of Pera.

"The departure of Murad gave way to long negotiations. The Turkish government demanded that he leave armless and under the police guard, but the Patriarchate did not accept the intervention of the officers, and Murad himself categorically refused to put his arms down. Finally the authorities finally gave in.

"In the morning Murad called for his comrades to go into the Assembly hall. They collected the necessary papers and divided them according to addresses. He stuck a dagger in his wide belt, checked his pistol, put it in his side pocket, and bidding farewell to all he left.

"Accompanying him were the famous secretary of the Patriarchate, Tiran Kelekian, and a priest, who went with him to the harbor from where he would board a Greek steamboat, the streets filled with Armenian parties and armed guards as well informants.

"Shortly after I received a letter from Murad from Athens, along with anti-drinking Hunchak ID cards to be distributed among the friends.

17

"I had kept these for a long time, as well as his gift, a small dagger.

"Years later, in Persia during the First World War, we suddenly learned about the escape of the hero from the Anatolian hell, the papers in Tbilisi and Baku describing in detail how Murad, with his instinctual suspicion, escaped being trapped by the Turks

"'I don't trust them,' he had been reported to have said, 'I will not part with my arms. I know Turks.'

"This reminded me of what he had said years back when he was leaving Kendronakan."

* * *

Another witness to the incidents in Constantinople, one of our patriotic clergy at the time, Rev. Mesrop Ter Mesropian, said the following about Murad in his memoirs:

"As the Archpriest of the Galatia church, I had the opportunity to work with the hero of Kovtun. Many of his relatives resided in Galatia, and I had received confessions from almost all of them. Before meeting Murad I had come to know all of them as selfless and devoted revolutionaries. Almost all of them were Hunchaks, which was the dominant political party at the outset of the revolution in Constantinople.

"From his adolescent years in Kovtun Murad had rebelled against the Turkish rule. He was constantly fighting with the Turks. His mother had to send him to Constantinople to her relatives, Khachik Agha Kralian. At that time, Khachik Agha's son, Grigor Kralian, also a revolutionary who was married and had five children, was under surveillance and would eventually die on the road in exile.

"One day, the Kralians brought their newly arrived young relative Murad to me. He was still a juvenile, medium height, chubby and strong with glowing face. Shortly after he created

Very Rev. Fr. Mesrop Mesropian,
former Pastor of the St. Illuminator Church, Galatia

an air of warmth around him. Despite his illiteracy and youth, both young and old had a special respect for him. Many from Sepastia gathered around him, revolutionaries from Kovtun in particular.

"Following the Bab Ali[27] demonstrations, the government intensified its persecutions, especially of the Armenians from the provinces who had settled in Constantinople, and it surrounded the Galatia, Beria, and Gum Gapu churches with spies and police.

"Despite the surveillance, the Hunchak leaders decided to take refuge in the churches and not leave without sufficient guarantees. The number of those taking refuge in the Galatia church was about four hundred and fifty. The Patriarch at the time was Izmirlian.

"This was a peaceful demonstration, aimed at alerting the European powers to the ongoing horrors and asking for their intervention. In fact the consuls of the five major powers visited Patriarch Izmirlian several times, and the British Consul paid him a visit almost daily to conduct negotiations. His interpreter was P. Mostichian, the principal of the Kendronakan School of Galatia.

"Our main concern was how to sustain such a large crowd night and day for weeks within the narrow quarters of the St. Lusavorich Church, preventing any eruption of disorder as well as feeding everyone. The supervision of Pera church was trusted to the Patriarch Abp. Eznik Apahuni, and to me of the Galatia church.

"It was during these days when the young revolutionary Murad manifested his organizational skills. A Board of Trustees that was organized under his guidance introduced military discipline among the crowd, and he took upon himself the task of the distributing food.

"Government spies often sneaked into the church confines, which on occasion led to numerous incidents. At Murad's orders these spies were subjected to meticulous interrogation and even corporal punishment and incarceration.

"Finally the ambassadors of the five powers visited the Galatia church one day, on which occasion it was covered with the black curtains of mourning, and those wishing to leave were issued ID cards stamped in the name of the ambassadors which presumably guaranteed their safety.

"The majority left, but seventy-two people refused, demanding the implementation of the promised reforms. Murad was one of the seventy-two.

"He had become a popular figure by then. People came from all over Constantinople to see him. Despite his modesty, the hero of Kovtun, despite his silence and his military discipline, wore a smile, which created an immediate connection between them and won the affection of even those unfamiliar with him.

"When we decided to send Murad and his comrades abroad there were lengthy negotiations. The government insisted in his disarming, but he refused, threatening to leave only by death.

"Eventually the means were found, and leaving in pairs day by day he and his comrades were led to a steamship waiting at the port. Murad was the last to leave after he was sure of his comrades' safe passage.

"Shortly thereafter, the Iron Patriarch was exiled to Jerusalem, and Archbishop Eznik and I were arrested. The Archbishop was sentenced to life imprisonment and I to a five-year sentence."

III

Murad in the Caucasus

After staying a few months in Egypt our hero left for Athens, where he witnessed with envy the relatively good condition of the Greek people and their impressive advances after winning independence. His heart however was filled with sadness about his own fatherland that was still under the yoke of a reactionary state, and the impression the Greeks made on him moved him further toward revolutionary struggle. And so he departed for the Caucasus accompanied by a friend, Karapet Mkhchian of Zeitun, to be closer to the developments in Turkish Armenia.

There he began calling for an Armenian emancipation that was to emanate from Van and Sasun and not Constantinople.

The Caucasus was new to him then. Arriving in Tbilisi and needing a livelihood he applied for a job at the Enfiachian Tobacco Company, where he was paid sixty *kopeks* a days for piling bales of the tobacco with a Georgian worker who had been there quite a while.

This Georgian worker was paid three times more than he, which bothered him, especially since he worked harder and was faster and stronger and smarter. At the same time this Georgian resented the Armenian's strength and efficiency and

*Murad 20-21 years old. His first photo after
joining the revolutionaries' ranks*

tried to have him fired by continually bad-mouthing him.
One day he suddenly attacked him and tried to prove his
strength by bringing him to the ground. Since Murad had
won the management's favor because of his good work, he
had patiently endured his fellow worker's jealousy, but this
surprise attack was the straw that broke the camel's back.

23

"If you want to prove your strength," he said, "let's step outside the factory and go to the park and wrestle."

The Georgian agreed and the fight took place in the garden. The owner of the factory, Enfiachian, watched the whole scene from his office. The Georgian was a well-built sport and the fight lasted for some time, gradually reaching its climax when Murad, who from childhood had been a skillful wrestler, threw his opponent down several times and finally knelt on his chest.

A voice from the factory office called, "Enough, Murad, enough."

Realizing there were spectators, the two wrestlers separated and left.

The Georgian, unable to endure his dishonor, eventually left the factory, and the victorious wrestler from Sepastia took his place. All the other workers congratulated him, and the owner of the factory even tripled his salary.

But none of this meant much to Murad. He had come to the Caucasus for something more important.

One day he suddenly left Tbilisi and headed toward Lori in the direction of an Armenian district at the Russian-Turkish border.

There was no railway then, nor did he have any money for a carriage, so he went on foot and arrived in Kars[26] in seven days. There he became acquainted with several people who introduced themselves as committee members of the Armenian Revolutionary Federation (A.R.F.).

"I have been a Hunchak until now," he told them, "but I see here a stronger organization with which I sympathize and would like to join on condition that I be dispatched with the first volunteers to the homeland."

The committee accepted. In those days A.R.F. units were being prepared to enter the homeland with arms for self-defense, and he joined them carrying rifles on his back across the border. From there they went to Gomadzor where they met another unit transporting arms for Sasun. He wanted to join this second group to Sasun, but he was not permitted, perhaps because he was new in the ranks and was not yet trusted.

He returned with his comrades to Kars,[28] hoping he would have another chance to go to Sasun, which had been the place of his dreams. Transporting arms was an indispensable mission, but he thirsted for confronting the enemy on the battlefield.

After his group returned to Kars, a second was dispatched to Gomadzor, and when the time came to pick a leader he was unanimously chosen to supervise the depot in Basen. In the meantime he continued to ask the Kars committee to let him join the fighting in Sasun.

There was always a call for reinforcements, and orders were received for a group to be dispatched for Sasun via Vaghar-shakert and Akhlat. With feverish preparation under way, Murad, confident that this time he would make it to Sasun, worked day and night preparing water jogs and back packs. There was a shortage of shells and rifles and resolving this problem also fell on his shoulders.

He was well known in the Kars region by now, having lived there for years, and thanks to his mild manners, modesty and warm voice, he had befriended everyone. The Armenian community knew he had left everything, both family and household, devoting himself to the cause of his people. Thus, trusted by everybody, he enjoyed their support. The Armenian soldiers of the Russian fortress provided him with shells and rifles and the women with clothing, shirts, socks, and woven gloves.

The departing transport group however left without Murad, and on the way they were caught in a skirmish, which brought the Turkish and Russian authorities face to face. Surveillance in Kars became even tighter and Murad was put under a strict watch by the Russian military. Then one day he was arrested and interrogated but set free from lack of sufficient evidence.

He then left Kars and crossed to the Russian-controlled side of Basen where he could be free from surveillance, and there he began his relentless propaganda activities, walking into the houses of the peasants and introducing them to the national cause and organizing fighting groups.

In early 1898 the [A.R.F.] Bureau received a letter from Sasun signed by Serob, the rebel leader of Nemrut, who was asking for weapons and ammunitions. The Eastern Bureau then ordered the Kars Committee to organize a convoy of a hundred people to transport them and Murad was again eager to go, but the Kars Committee again did not grant him permission. He was considered indispensable to the Kars region, not only to spread liberation propaganda and organize units, but also to neutralize the spies and traitors.

Then came the Kristapor's[29] days of The Storm,[30] and the wealthy Armenians finally had to open their coffers for the national liberation cause, otherwise this would have been done by force. This was one of the most difficult and grave tasks of the A.R.F., to bring the Armenian wealthy class to its senses and make it see its duty to the nation.

Murad was in Tbilisi at the time and he participated fully in these operations. By order of Kristapor and with notices of The Storm in his pockets, he approached the Armenian gentry of Tbilisi and with his diplomacy enticed large sums from them.

IV

Sasun

Upon completing The Storm operation, Murad resolved to enter Turkey at any cost. The sounds of alarm had been heard again from Sasun, and the Turkish government was determined to remove once and for all the nest of freedom fighters. They had taken refuge in the high mountains, feverishly preparing for the unavoidable confrontation and sending requests to the Eastern Bureau in the Caucasus for fresh fighting units and arms and ammunition.

In May 1903 Torgom's group, which had already encountered many battles, left for Sasun, and Murad joined them as a common soldier. Arriving in Sasun they found Hrayr, Vahan Toghramachian, Andranik, Makar, Gevorg Chavush, Seyto, Mshetsi, Smbat, Shenektsi, Manuk, Sepuh, Keri, Vagharshak, Kaytsak Arakel, and Avo of Trebizond, all of whom would become honored in the history of our liberation movement.

After the Hamidian massacres[31] of 1895-1896, a generation of fighters seemed to have expired. Many thought the liberation movement had fired its last shells in the 1896 Vaspurakan fights and that the three Armenian parties with their Petos, Martiks and Avetisians were all finished. The bells of St. Bartholomew[32] seemed to toll the wake of the revolution itself.

But this was not to be the case. Although the branches of our tree were severed our trunk still stood with its roots remaining to nurture new sprouts.

"Old roots and new branches will give rise to another Armenian realm."

Ghevond Alishan.

And the largest of these branches would be the elite of the great Taron, some of whose members were battle-hardened warriors.

It was a new harvest of heroes, as the poet Schiller might say, a *Heroensaat* [crop of heroes] who were to reverse our losses, in particular the tragic one of Aghbiwr Serob.[33] Zealous and brave, they seemed like the legendary princes of the mountains come to life in the battle for a new fatherland. They had come together with relatively favorable political conditions and they would be crowned with fame like the great characters of a Greek epic, Botsaris and Miaullis.[34] But a ruthless Russian diplomacy would eventually put an end to their goal, and their eagle's nest would be razed and leveled to the ground.

These fighters had been the elite of Sasun: Hrayr, Chavush, Kaytsak, Vahan, Avo, Manuk, Andranik, Vagharshak, Murad, Sepuh, Galeh, Makar, and many others. The heavens seemed to have usurped them from their ancestral homeland, depriving them of earthly pleasures and plunging them into an abyss, but they were fierce fighters in whose hearts blazed the eternal flame of revenge, especially for those traitors who had betrayed Serob and destroyed their homes. How fearsome was the scene when they surrounded and killed the dreadful Khalil after interrogating and torturing him.

* * *

Standing from left to right Sepuh, Andranik, Murad

They were ruthless souls, yes, and they were even more ruthless with their own kind. With Spartan self-denial and fierce discipline, they could be merciless toward their own pain.

One of Murad's friends told the following incident concerning Hajji Koto, who after one of the Sasun battles crossed into Persia along with Murad and Andranik.

"During the fighting a Turkish bullet had pierced Murad's index finger and severed the tip of it. The wound healed but the bone was exposed and was painful when it touched anything. With him was Eghiazar of Khoy, who had returned from America and had practiced medicine, and he said the wound had to be opened and the bone amputated.

"And so without chloroform or any other anesthetics our hero sat firmly on a chair, pulled out a red handkerchief from his pocket, folded it several times and put it in his mouth, then he extended his hand to the astonished doctor and said, 'Do your job.'"

Gevorg Chavush

Such was the passion of our warriors who became drunk with the sword and rifle and the smell of gun powder,[35] not only Murad but Chavush, Avo, Keri, Andranik, Seydo, Galeh Makar and so many others.

They had been uneducated village men, and yet they schooled themselves in the art of war with strategies and tactics as advanced as those taught in the military academies of the most advanced nations.

Their leader, Andranik himself, had been in 1897 a common soldier during the campaign of Khanasor under the command of Vazgen, but few years later he took over from the great Serob.

Malkhas of Trabzon, who had lived for years in Vaspurakan and was trusted with many responsibilities at the Turco-Per-

Hrayr Dzhoghk (né Armenak Ghazarian, 1866-1904)

sian border and Transcaucasus, has given us a description of the survivors of Sasun, who after the battle in 1904 crossed into Vaspurakan with Andranik and from there marched to Persia.[36]

"I went to greet them with two soldiers. Their caravan was at the side of the road and it was cold and they were resting and warming themselves around a fireplace and Andranik was with them.

"Then in the dark of night we came to my humble residence in the Khoy which was the home of the Dashnaktsutiwn.

"I had never come across such a venerable group of men. To me they were titans, each one no less than the other. There was an astonishing harmony among them, filled with compassion for each other.

"The central figure among them was Andranik, and it has to be said that it was he who initiated the jokes to lighten their souls, inducing them to tease each other. Then there would be bursts of joyous laughter, and I would leap with mirth as if to the 'ninth sky.'

"There was in this group a unique hero, Murad of Sepastia, who was not only jovial and dynamic, but had a thoughtful face that left me with the impression of the god Vahagn.

"There was also Kaytsak [thunder] Arakel, and the mercurial Agha, the group's eldest revolutionary, who had begun his fight with Keri of Erzincan even before the 1890s.

"The other jewels of this group were Sepuh and Arshak of Baberd, the latter reminding me of Kiklop of the Odysseus, who was an old, seasoned veteran and who had worn out his youth on the road. Among them Sepuh was the most literate, and he even wrote poetry which actually was quite good.

"Seydo-Poghos of Mush, no less prominent, was also with them. An ordinary person in daily life, he would become very brave during the fighting, the bullets firing past as if from a machine gun. He would later fall victim in the Kurdish-Armenian action.

"There was also modest Avo the *Barmakhsz*,[37] who knew nothing but the revolution and the tasks assigned to him. He never sought glory, though he deserved it and should now be acknowledged.

"One of the youngest was Smbat of Mush, whose chest was decorated with a long silver *kerotik*.[38] He too was a brave soldier who, after the fighting in Sasun, contributed his share of heroism during the days of the republic. An injury to his head left half his body paralyzed. Later, during the February [1921] revolt, he was again present with his comrades from Mush.

"Among the others were Mnjo, Hajji Gevo, Aslan, Zarab Arshak, and Hajji Koto in particular."

* * *

They would all be killed except two who though in exile now are part of our community here in America.

Arriving at the mountain highland of his dreams, Murad, the former insurgent of Constantinople, increased his extraordinary activities with unprecedented zeal. The people of Sasun and his new comrades loved him, and he soon became one of the pillars of the organization, studying every corner of the country and its heights and valleys and ravines, encouraging his comrades with his warmth and honesty.

Prior to the 1904 revolt, some of them wanted to appoint him leader, but he refused, recommending instead Andranik who after the death of Serob had already been leading a group of insurgents.

"Our leader is Andranik," Murad said, "and if he dies we will carry his body with our banner in our battle for freedom."

Not everybody liked Andranik, whose coarse behavior could be irritating and offensive, and yet, everybody agreed with Murad and Vahan's words of encouragement, and so Andranik became their leader.

Murad was elected a member of the Military Council, but never interfered in the decision of the commander general's decisions.

When the Turks were preparing for an attack on the Armenian citadel, Murad descended into the plain of Mush and stayed there a few months, traveling through the villages and sounding the alarm for everyone to face the impending danger while organizing their self-defense. And the people embraced him, who seemed to personify the spirit of the campaign. Thus, many of the peasants did sell their belongings and oxen and cattle to purchase arms. Murad in the meantime trained the youth how to use them.

A winter passed with their waiting and when spring arrived in 1904, the storm erupted.

Turkish forces came from as far away as Diarbekir, circling Sasun and cutting all communication between the mountains and the plain. The peasants were searched and the Muslim mob was incited against the Armenians to disarm and terrorize them

At the same time the enemy tried to calm opinion among the Europeans. It had come to finish the task left incomplete after the massacres of 1894-1896, to annihilate the entire Armenian population of Sasun and Taron, but it was also extremely worried about what was in progress in Europe. It worried about the fierce resistance of the people of Sasun, so it advanced with large contingents, steadily and cautiously, avoiding risky moves and large-scale massacres, even at the plain of Mush where it would have been relatively easy to carry out such a measure. It wanted to show the world that it had come to punish the Armenian "rebels" in Sasun, to which no one could object.

Even when the Turkish army, after lengthy preparations, ascended to Sasun with mountain cannons, there too it did not resort to major military operations. It did not want to be seen taking preemptive and proactive measures. Instead it slowly prepared the grounds for an easy victory, succeeding again to instigate the Kurdish tribes against the Armenians, while the efforts of the Dashnaktsutiwn to neutralize this were to no avail.

The Kurdish conspiracies erupted in various corners. In Tapeka they tried to encircle and trap Andranik and kill him, but they were foiled and punished by our boys.

The repercussions in Tavale and Gom were heavier. The Kurds of Patkan decided to attack seven Armenian homes in that region and capture their belongings and take hostages, but an Armenophile Kurd betrayed his comrades. The villages of Shenik and Semal were agitated. Murad at that time was in Semal. He called a meeting and after consultations he went overnight with Iso of Gomer and Israel Mokunts and to free the seven Armenian households.

It was the day before Easter, March 27, 1904. He was about to leave when the news arrived that the Kurds had attacked Talave and looted the house of Mirbo. They had taken Mirbo's son and imprisoned the rest of the Armenians in their homes.

Murad headed to Tavale with his comrades and razed the homes of the Kurds and saved a number of the abducted Armenians, then retreated to Kelieknman and took positions there. The news spread among the Kurds and about two hundred of their fighters attacked the Armenian positions. A bloody fight ensued on March 30.

The Armenians of Shenik and Selam came to the help of Murad's group and the fight lasted from dawn to noon. It ended with a devastating defeat of the Kurds, Murad and his comrades and the people of Sasun manifesting exceptional bravery and heroism.

After showing fierce resistance, the enemy began to retreat. At that point Murad ordered a ceasefire to save ammunition. "This is just the beginning," he said. Just then an enemy shot brought down *Hayduk*[39] Eeso, one of the best fighters of the group. Murad was outraged and swore on the corpse of his fallen comrade to avenge his death. Leading his group, he pursued the retreating enemy, and in the Kurdish village of Lachkan another fight erupted in which many Kurds and Turks were killed and a number of villages were plundered.

Shortly after they took the body of their fallen comrade and returned to Shenik, where they waited for new developments. They held a meeting in Semal with the lords of Sasun and Talvorik, and then the fighting units were dispatched in various directions, each with specific instructions.

Murad was to defend the Kurtuk Mountain, which was the most important point in the area, in regard to Kope and Shushanamerk and the advance of the enemy reinforcements.

The powerful counterattack of Armenian fighters worried the Turkish government, who tried to resort to its usual deception to cut their losses. In late March 1904, by the order of the *Vali*[40] of Bitlis, Vardapet Arakel came to Sasun to conduct negotiations with the rebels. He had with him an encyclical issued by the Patriarch Ormanian and a decree issued by the Sultan that promised to grant amnesty to all the fedayees if they turned in their weapons and surrendered, otherwise Sasun would be attacked by a regular army with cannons.

Murad, who was part of the military council, categorically declared that no revolutionary could accept such demeaning conditions. "We are ready to sacrifice our lives in these mountains and never surrender to the enemy alive."

Shortly after, the Turkish army, which had already surrounded Sasun with cannons, began bombarding the positions of the fedayees.

The entire mountain slope shook under the shelling and the incessant and deafening roar of machine guns. Bodies fell on both side on the slope and rolled into the ravines. Murad kept moving from one position to another under the barrage, and the fedayees' own barrage did not let the enemy advance. The resistance was successful as long as there was sufficient ammunition, but when the supplies dried up, the situation became critical. It was impossible to defend against a Turkish army of about 20,000 who had been joined by a large number of Kurdish brigands.

The Armenian fighters gradually retreated to the mountain heights in the direction of Antok, taking with them the local population.

One after another, these heights were surrounded by the Turkish army. The Armenians held out until the last shell was fired, after which they had no other choice but to descend to the plains in order to escape unavoidable massacre. They descended while simultaneously fighting the enemy that had swarmed over the entire area. There were several fights in the plains where the Armenians were able to find some ammunition and food and inflict heavy casualties on the enemy. Let us recall the battle of Kurava with a description from the *Droshak*.[41]

"One day, on July 17, 1904, news came that the Turkish army had entered the village of Kurava and began making demands. A Turkish soldier tried to rape an Armenian woman who screamed and escaped. The fedayees, Andranik, Murad, and Arakel, along with their fighters watched the events from their hiding posts. They were divided into four groups. A Turkish soldier approached the door where Arakel's company was located, and when he saw them through the cracks of the door he alarmed his comrades, '*Keyin burda fedayee var*' Keyin there is a fedayee here.'

"Shortly after the house was surrounded. Watching this, the other units waited until more Turkish soldiers assembled so that their bullets could have a bigger harvest.

"Suddenly our boys rained fire from three directions and Turkish bodies fell on top of one another. There was confusion and some of them barely managed to take positions behind the village and the cemetery. Shouting revenge Murad and his comrades stormed the cemetery from two directions and a fierce battle ensued, almost face-to-face. Smbat, Iso, Poghos, and Astur came to his help. With enemy bodies covering the cemetery, the survivors somehow escaped with their commander.

"The fedayees had to hide because Turkish reinforcements would soon appear. Ordered by Andranik, Murad went to inform the other fedayees to assemble on the banks of the Murad River. Then hidden by the night they crossed the river and disappeared in the darkness."

Murad, Andranik, Sepuh and other comrades, Persia [Iran], 1904

The rest is well known. Our boys never believed they could defeat the Turks with such unequal forces. They banked their hopes on foreign intervention. In fact the British and French consuls had come to Mush by order of their governments to observe the Turkish troop movements. They were waiting for the arrival of the Russian consul to take more serious measures, but he did not show up and time kept dragging on. When he finally came it was too late. Like ten years before, during the days of [Alexey Borisovich] Lobanov-Rostovsky,[42] Russia would take a treacherous course in the Armenian tragedy.

However the goal of the Turks did not materialize this time either. True, the Armenians of Sasun suffered losses in 1903 and 1904, but they were still in revolt. Their masses everywhere, even on the plain of Mush, had survived sporadic massacres. They owed this largely to the popular movements in the West who were in their favor, in particular the *Pro Arme-*

nia[43] agitation of French sympathizers who raised the Armenian Question in the Parliament. These compatriots demanded the *Déclassé* administration watch over the Armenocidal policies of the Turks and warn the leaders in the Yildiz Kioshk[44] to appoint new consuls in the endangered locations.

The Armenian Question was put before the Western powers and public opinion rose sharply as a result of the events in Sasun. However, Tsarist Russia, the government most concerned with the fate of Armenia, once again was not in concert with the West, since the weakening of Armenia would be beneficial to her.

Yet it also has to be said that even Russia, influenced by Europe and in particular the Armenophile movement in France, did not encourage yet another large scale massacre.

* * *

The turbulent days of Sasun became history, and though Sultan Hamid continued to plan of the complete annihilation of the Armenians, no major event took place until the Ottoman revolutionary period of 1908, not even after the 1905 explosion of Yildiz, which was aimed at the Sultan himself. The Armenian Revolutionary Federation had succeeded in swaying public opinion in Europe under whose supervision the executioner's hand had been stayed.

Turkish Armenia was still alive, although plundered and bloodstained. The Armenian homeland was still alive, and it gradually began to recover and rebuild and bury the tragic days of the Hamid. It would have gradually strengthened if the First World War did not erupt, which would once and for all sever Turkey from Europe and provide ground for the greatest tragedy in Armenian history.

Sasun was still alive, but gone were her leaders, Hrayr and Vahan, who had been killed during the fight. Murad and his comrades had crossed the Caucasus into Persia. Andranik had gone to rest and to meet the Western Bureau [of the A.R.F.] in Geneva, where he would stay for a year and a half and write his memoir of his fifteen-years as a partisan. But Murad and his inseparable comrades Sepuh, Kaytsak, and Avo stayed in the Caucasus where a new period of fights and sacrifices had begun on the Russian Armenian stage, a year and a half long stormy era known as the Armeno-Tatar war.[45]

V

Murad and Andranik

There are many parallels between the two prominent figures of the Armenian revolutionary movement, though they are so different from each other.

Allow me to view some of these parallels, since both are deceased and are now part of history and thus subject to comparison. Both can be commended in regard to bravery and self-sacrifice and neither surpasses the other in gallantry and fearlessness.

The senior was an experienced commander and strategist, while Murad was endowed with unusual physical strength and intelligence and had more knowledge of military and civilian affairs. He was perhaps even more accustomed to the harsh and bitter conditions of life. Both were rustic and plain in character, with no formal education and yet eloquent in speech. Had they been in more fortunate conditions, they undoubtedly would have become first-rate orators or writers.

By nature Andranik was rough and cocky in regard to rules and regulations. Murad, on the contrary, was disciplined and friendly, frank, open hearted, warm and modest, but sometimes also withdrawn.

Shant's group

Two years after the events in Sasun, in the summer of 1906, when Zangezur[46] and Russian Armenia were engulfed by the fire of the Turkish-Armenian clashes, astounding news arrived in Tbilisi about the bloody battles in Ghapan and the victorious march of the warrior of Sepastia against the Turks, and it captured the people's imagination. One day as we were sitting at the editorial offices of *Haraj*[47] with Avetis Aharonian,[48] joyfully recording the news of the Armenian victories, the door suddenly opened and a well-built soldier of medium height and dressed in the fatigues of a freedom fighter entered the room. Stepping care-free with a nice smile on his face, he greeted us and stood by the wall with his hands down like a disciplined student in a classroom.

It was Murad himself.

He did not take a chair until we invited him to sit.

I felt full of joy. I had just come to Geneva and had not seen this famous leader.

I asked insatiably about the battles in Zangezur and his accomplishments, not only to satisfy my curiosity but because it was essential for the issues of the party organ. But it proved futile, since he did not want to speak about himself.

"Okay Murad dear, let's hear it," I said.

"Oh, Mikayel, we struck and they fled."

And then he moved to another topic.

My second meeting with him was in Constantinople in the summer of 1911 during the World Congress of A.R.F. I repeated my questions there too, but he was getting ready to return to his birthplace in Sepastia.

The third and last time was in Tbilisi in 1915, when after his agony I embraced him farewell, since I was preparing to leave for abroad. I pleaded with him again that like Andranik he should write his memoirs or at least dictate them to someone, but once again he gave me the same answer like a shy and bashful kid.

"Oh Mikayel, that is not important."

Andranik, on the contrary, had a great need to include himself in history. In late 1904, when he came to Geneva his first concern was to draft an extensive memoir of his life at the editorial offices of the *Droshak*. He took one of our young comrades and for months dictated to him the stories of his battles and adventures.

We did not think this was a bad idea. I wish all our warriors and intellectual leaders had the same concerns. Andranik's memoir is very valuable, though he had the tendency to assert that without his participation no important event would have transpired. He tended to place himself at the center of events, often at the expense of others, and even to embellish his persona while disparaging others, including the deceased.

Andranik was full of contradictions (*esprit de contradiction*), bold, independent, and extremely individualistic. He would rarely accept the requests and suggestions of his comrades without going through lengthy and tiring arguments.

Andranik

Often in the gravest of moments he would drop everything and seclude himself like a mischievous child, making his comrades appeal to him time and again. He rarely accepted disagreement as a matter of principle. The force controlling him was glory and he refused to recognize any authority but to work freely and independently. Such was the reason why he was constantly criticized and blamed.

But it is also true that Andranik was compassionate toward his soldiers. In spite of his rough and dictatorial manner, he took care of them like a caring father. He also liked the Armen-

44

ian working class and detested all its enemies, including the unfaithful and calcified and irresponsible Armenian wealthy.

He was moody as well. However, if he felt good—a rare occasion—and in a warm and friendly circle, he could be absolutely captivating with his thoughtful and sweet conversation and kind smile, his vibrant voice mixing with bursts of laughter.

As a general rule he did not like intellectuals, but he did like strong military leaders. Among them were Eprem and Duman who mesmerized him, the former especially, who was the great commander of the Persian liberation movement and whose life he studied fervently. It was said that he also studied the life of Napoleon in whom perhaps he wanted to see some mutual traits.

In general, especially after some victorious campaigns in 1915, for which he was decorated with the St. George medal of the Tsarist government, his fighter's soul took on an aura of megalomania, a fever which would one day drive him against his commander, General [Thovmas] Nazarbekian, and even against his country's own legitimate government. He felt as if he embodied the Armenian spirit itself in all its glory and power, and yet how damaged his character became with his fame and charm. There is no real greatness without the humility and modesty like that of such heroes as Eprem, Serob, Duman and Murad.

Military genius is a great thing, but not enough for history, which wants to also record a man's behavior and personality. If [Ferdinand] Foch[49] is honored today in his French homeland more than Napoleon, it might be because Foch as well as being a military genius was also a marvelous personality and a man of exceptional qualities, above all modesty and humility.

Murad lacked Andranik's negative tendencies and because of this his comrades loved him passionately.

On one side was the illustrious warrior and on the other a good citizen.

Yet the great son of Sepastia was not just an affable lamb, he too on occasion could roar like a tiger.

"Bold and meek" said Shakespeare about one of his heroes, and so too was our man from Kovtun with his mixed bag of two opposing tendencies. At times he was a lamb, and at others a tiger. Such was he like in the streets of Constantinople when he terrorized the Armenian "moths," or in the heights of Sasun and Ghapan when he pursued the Tatar hordes, as well as in times of peace during the struggles in Party meetings.

However, even in moments of outrage he knew how to keep the balance worthy of a citizen. He did not rebel against the discipline or the regulations of law and order.

"Masculine and alert was that amazing Sepastian," wrote Avetis Aharonian in his article entitled *Andranik*.[50]

"I do not remember anyone of our revolutionary fighters to have left such a deep and total impression on me like Murad of Sepastia," continued the bard of the Armenian freedom battle and one of its heroes. "Even as I write these lines he is before my eyes with his bronze body and his fiery eyes and thick eyebrows, his impressive head on a masculine neck exuding power and nobility, his mane of thick black hair that made him look like a lion, his massive arms that could control the most wild horses. No one could ride a horse that Murad had tamed. His steps were firm and steady, and when he walked it seemed as if the earth was trembling.

"How mesmerizing and thought provoking were his conversations. Open-minded and clear thinking, he could debate with any orator, sociologist, or literary critic, always adding with a kind smile that 'we are the men of the people and illiterate peasants, so please forgive us for our trespasses.'

"Oh, Murad, the Armenian people in its endless list of losses and sorrow does not have enough time to bow her head for her fallen children."

During the Mihranian movement[51] the troubled days of 1906, when a deep dissension split the ranks of the organization, Murad was wholeheartedly with Mihran, like almost all the Western Armenian leaders, and despite staying in the party he rattled his sword against the socialist and separatist youths who demanded the Dashnaktsutiwn leave the cause of Turkish Armenia to Turkish Armenians and engage exclusively with the fate of the Caucasian Armenians in harmony with Russian socialism.

I remember well those unforgettable spring days of the A.R.F. General Assembly in Vienna in 1907, when I was in the presence of Andranik, Sepuh, Vardan, Sako, Rostom, Zawarian, Ishkhan of Van, Aknuni, Aharonian, Hamo Ohanjanian, Shahkhatunian and many others. Murad roared against the Dashnaktsutiwn's anti-Mihranian leaders and threatened bloodshed if the separatist were not expelled from the ranks. It was the unfortunate Eghishe Topchian who responded to Murad sharply and was himself the first to fall by his brother Mihran's bullets on the road from Trabzon to Erzurum two years after the Vienna meeting. In those days Murad had been dragged into radicalism, which had some failing steps and pitfalls.

However, the hayduk, the warrior of Sepastia, despite sympathizing with Mihran in matters of principle, stayed away from this agent of the Russian police and did not approve of his behavior. Contrary to his fiery speeches, he never took active steps against the socialist youth of Caucasian Armenia. He never touched a hair of a Dashnaktsakan.[52]

Eventually his discipline and modesty won over his comrades. They finally saw through the Arakelians and other fanatical anti-Dashnakatsakans and that Mihran had fallen into the claws of a Tsarist conspiracy and had become an informer and a traitor. They turned away from the Mihranian strikes and after the deaths of Mihran, Shkhali and other sympathizers, they all remained in the ranks of Dashnaktsutiwn [A.R.F.]. Thus, the A.R.F. was saved from serious disintegration, which had been the goal of its real enemy, the Tsarist government.

Undoubtedly Murad, with his awareness and discipline, played a role in this counter-movement. He soon became convinced that the socialist youth were as sincerely devoted to the Armenian cause as were the Turkish Armenians. The so-called separatists too, with the exception of the late Levon Atabekian and a few of his comrades, returned to the bosom of the Mother Party.

They all retained their positions. Only Andranik was to depart at the end of the Great War, which was solely due to personal reasons that I will not deal with here. He was to fall into the bosom of opposing elements who had accused Armenian fighters of being adventurous brigands and nation slayers. This was a true desecration.[53]

Thus were the two figures, Andranik and Murad: one always hungrily looking for applause, the other always staying in the shadow, one out of petty egoism and the other proud but modest that he was able to serve the great cause.

Andranik's presence would often put his comrades in a tense situation. They knew that he could become bitter or capable of bold gestures that something could easily erupt. But when Murad entered a meeting, however, he would with his smile create a pleasant and calming atmosphere. Andranik with his thunderous looks could on the other hand become theatrical, which would impress an unruly crowd and keep the ranks in fear and submission.

One day in Tbilisi [capital of Georgia] he entered the hall of the [Armenian] National Bureau with his arms when about twenty-five of the deputies were presided by Spendarian and consulting an urgent issue.

Taking a chair he disrupted the meeting and giving himself the right to speak he talked about everything but what was on the agenda, criticizing and even mocking those present. He talked incessantly for two hours, despite appeals by the president, until the meeting was adjourned and he had wasted its precious time.

I recall also another occasion when he created a commotion in Vladikavkaz. It was in 1916 when he had been invited to be honored as a national hero at a reception. I did not hide my feelings and had opposed this, but our compatriots of Vladikavkaz decided to invite him anyway, along with Russians, Ossets, Chechens, Ingush and others.

It was an extraordinary demonstration. I had rarely seen such an intense manifestation of fascination and gratitude toward a national hero as that of the people of the beautiful Vladikavkaz, that was founded by Loris-Melikov[54] and had such a large Armenian community. Armenians owned almost all the automobiles and they drove through the main streets to the railway station with the rest going there on foot. The entire station was crammed with the young and the old to greet the Armenian general whose fame was known through the Armenian and non-Armenian press and who had been decorated with the Georgian medal. The local Russian papers published salutary articles about him, and for a moment even I got excited by the scene and felt anxious for the opposition.

Then came the moment when the idol descended from a car accompanied by two bodyguards, looking as he always did on such occasions. He was like an Eastern patriarch, a Persian Shah, a Chinese Mandarin, solemn and glorious. The impression on the crowd was immense and a religious silence overcame them with misty eyes, and then came the applause and the hurrahs. The Armenian priest came forward and made a speech in the name of the local public and to extend greetings.

But the priest had barely uttered a word when Andranik gestured insultingly and ignored him. The poor priest did not deserve to be subjected to such an insult before the entire community. He too was once a warrior. He was Father Hakob Sarikian of the Khanasor.

It was as if cold water had been splashed on the scene and the crowd was stunned. However the wave of jubilation did not subside, and the air would once again be filled with applause and "Long live Andranik!"

Then came the entourage with Andranik in an automobile with his body guards, followed by a long line of others and the sea of people, all heading through the main street to the largest hotel in the city. There a Russian greeted him and read an address in the name of the Russian liberal elements. Fortunately everything was concluded peacefully without any incidents or derogatory gestures from Andranik.

A large crowd of enthusiasts of different nationalities and classes had assembled before the hotel for the apotheosis of their hero. Lucky were those who in such a time could keep their balance of mind without succumbing to such intoxication. Unfortunately, however, most could not.

The next day there was a huge banquet and taking part in it were the Russian-speaking Armenians whose excitement and enthusiasm was as great as that of the others, each one bringing a contribution to the volunteer movement.

It was a strange atmosphere when everybody took his place at the luncheon table. An oppressive silence seemed to overcome the reception hall. No one dared to ask a question or exchange words with the honored guest. Hundreds watched with silent fascination as he sat motionless with crossed eyebrows staring at the air, which was a bad omen.

A Russian-speaking Armenian with a low voice said, "He looks very serious."

The luncheon continued for some time in this atmosphere of theatrical silence. Then the toasts began. The same old battle-hardened fedayees priest, Sarikian, mustered all his power and began with extraordinary bravery a new welcome speech. Andranik, sitting next to me, began to make impatient moves. I was afraid that something was going to happen. Fortunately he listened until the priest finished, then he stood up and began to deliver in length his own speech, the gist of which was that the Armenians of Vladikavkaz were guilty of not fulfilling their duty to the national volunteer movement during the tragic periods. Thus did he rain his sharp comments on those present, but his accusations were exaggerated and out of place. After all, there is a way for saying such things. The hall was overcome with confusion and Sarikian glanced horrified in my direction.

When Andranik's barrage of accusations continued, some could no longer endure them and left the hall. Thus was the luncheon concluded and people left with grave impressions.

I would like to believe that the poses and gestures of the great warrior were just irrepressible eruptions of outrage. However they were often also fake and artificial. The applause and the *hosannas*[55] had gone to his head to such an extent that he thought of himself a moral philosopher and the *kharazan* (whip) of the Armenian nation.

* * *

From 1915 onwards the commander of the forces in Sasun made an unfortunate number of critical errors that would tarnish his name, and one had to see Murad's disappointment when, as early as 1916, he arrived in Tbilisi from Sepastia and learned of this. The scorpion of Sepastia was like a boy who had lost his elder brother.

"We worshipped that man," he said, "I do not understand how he could have changed that much?"

He questioned all his comrades about Andranik, and from every corner he heard the same painful view that weighed on his heart like a nightmare.

But truly impressive was the discipline and loyalty of our noble soldier regarding Andranik as his leader. And not only Murad, but also the other comrades who had fought under Andranik and accepted his military authority after the Sasun revolt. Let us remember Murad's harangue on the eve of that revolt when they were to choose a leader and when his own candidacy had strong supporters.

"Andranik is our leader," he had said, "Andranik is our successor to Serop, and even if he himself were dead, his spirit would march with our battle flag toward freedom."

And not only were they loyal to their chief they revered him.

Even Sepuh.

One day in 1921 we had gathered in a chapel in London where an Armenian priest was conducting a service for the local community, and present were the president of the Delegation of the Armenian republic, Avetis Aharonian, Armen Garo, Sepuh, Khatisian and myself. Andranik too was there, whose relations with Dashnaktsutiwn had been soured for some time. Also sour were his relations with Sepuh, who had just returned from the Caucasus.

They had not talked for some time. Sepuh had been upset by his actions and it seemed that their relations had been severed for good. But when the service was concluded and Andranik, along with his entourage, began to walk toward the door, Sepuh, as if hypnotized by Andranik's demeanor, greeted him and saluted. Andranik barely responded and extended his hand reluctantly, without pausing a moment except to say *goroz u vez* (arrogant) and continue on his way.

The scene reminded me of his pomposity in Vladikavkaz where he acted like an oriental dictator, particularly when he felt he was under the eyes of the public.

Yet here is what Sepuh wrote to Andranik in a letter dated May 5, 1906:[56]

"Dear Paruyr,[57]

"We are all ready to sacrifice our lives to your first and last command, for which we keep waiting."

Such was his loyalty, which tells us of Andranik's indisputable military skill.

Murad himself emphasized this in his brief reply to Avetis Aharonian.

"I once asked Murad," Aharonian wrote,[58] "in what sense was Andranik a chief, when none of his other comrades were no less than him." He did not appreciate my question. 'My friend, what a question,' he said. 'He is a leader. After all somebody has to lead so others will obey and follow. So, he was the most suitable.' And wanting to drop the subject he said let's go for a stroll, but I did not let him off the hook.

"Why, when he is not any braver than the rest of you? I said.

"'My friend,' he said, smiling, 'it is not just bravery that counts. Andranik has an insight which we do not.'

"Now it was my turn to smile, since this was not clear for me.

"'Why do you smile?' he said. 'I am telling the truth. Andranik has insight, and I am not making this up. When we crossed carelessly over the mountains and gorges with our rifles on our shoulders he noticed things that we didn't, he examined everything, every cliff and hill and grove and brook, and nothing escaped his eyes. And once he noticed something he never forgot it. If we were fighting in retreat, he would know full well how far we should pull back to reach a designated cliff or hill or mountain or ravine. Furthermore, he knew how to take the best positions against the enemy, under which cliff or behind which hill. Once he assigned our positions before a fight, we knew for sure it was the best, and in fact he was never wrong. Our fighting might last a whole day, but our position would remain the best. Fighting under his command was like a dance or a game. Once again I am telling you he had true insight in those moments.'

Thus, in the words of Aharonian, we can see even Murad's view of the leader's skill. I wish the commander himself could have been as respectful in return.

Nevertheless Murad was deeply disappointed and saddened by Andranik's mistakes. The great fedayee of Shabin Karahisar gravely damaged his reputation when in 1917 he dissented and fought against his mother-party by establishing the *Hayastan* paper in Tbilisi, which was a new separatist attempt and would be aborted like the first one.

Then came the sad days of Erzurum, when his bold failures also tarnished his military fame. Those were the stormy and fateful days of 1918 when he rebelled against the commander-in-chief of the Armenian army, General Nazarbekian, and a few months later moved with his soldiers from Ejmiatsin in the direction of Erevan against the government of Armenia. It seemed then that Napoleon's words had come true again: "The distance between greatness and failure is only a step."

This same brigand, this glorious conqueror of Dilman, brought his own downfall with his megalomania, then left his country on the eve of a new catastrophe and went abroad.

But let no one think we are trying to denigrate our national hero. No one has loved Andranik more than we, and his death caused great sorrow among his former comrades. However, as historians we must present all the facts, even those that pain us. We must do this so future generations will not forget that serving one's nation involves not only genius and bravery but respect for one's comrades and one's national institutions.

Four years have passed since the demise of our hero. The moss has long grown on his tomb, and may the spirit of the warrior which hovers over the cemetery at Père Lachaise[59] forgive us in recording not only his glories but also the less glorious facts of his turbulent career. May he forgives us, because he too welcomed criticism when he wrote in his memoirs about his two great comrades, Hrayr and Serob, who were also the pride of Armenian history.

The moral capital of Andranik's past is so immense that it can endure criticism. The Party, which he had carelessly bad mouthed, never responded to him in the same way. When the news of his death swept through the Diaspora, the reaction was almost the same as when Garibaldi died in Italy, fifty years ago today. Everybody mourned. The Dashnaktsutiwn walked with a huge cortège behind his hearse, and his former comrades encircled his remains with respect. Even Sepuh, who had been so harshly criticized by him, bowed before his casket.

Andranik, despite his failures and shortcomings, will be remembered as one of the greatest of warriors in Armenian history, shrouded with legend and immortality like Murad, Serob, Duman, Eprem, Hrayr, Gevorg, Keri, Aram, Ishkhan, and so many other giants of the sacred oath who shine like stars.

VI

In the Armeno-Tatar Clashes

On the walls of the St. Thaddeus Monastery and its neighboring buildings in the historic province of Artaz, inscribed in graphite and metal scratches. are the graffiti of the names of more than seven hundred Armenians, who, in the course of liberation movements, have marched through or taken refuge there.[60]

From Vaspurakan to Persia and back, both fighters and refugees had come and gone through this monastery, and even now visitors inscribe their names and dates of visit. Andranik's group also followed this tradition when he crossed from Sasun to Vaspurakan and then to Persia. The following is from Murad's own recording in his clear pencil script:

> *"Murad Sebastatsi*
> *"1904 – August (the day erased)*
> *"We crossed through fire and water, and I would also add through blood, yet we continued toward more fire and blood . . ."*[61]

It was true, new battles were in store for him, this time in Russian Armenia, which were to immortalize him in the hearts of the Armenians there. Those battles would be in the Armeno-Tatar war in 1905-1906.

In 1905, in the vast Russian empire from Finland to Poland to the Caucasus, a turbulent and unprecedented liberation movement would involve millions of people against the dictatorial regime of the Tsar. It originated from the massive strikes and popular demonstrations and terrorist acts as early as 1901, then it reached its climax toward the end of the Russo-Japanese war [of 1905] and the resounding defeat of the empire.

The two progressive nations of the Caucasus, Armenia and Georgia, were also swallowed in this revolutionary movement and even became the theaters for bloody battles. The Armenians happened to be the first to raise the banner of revolt as early as 1903, in response to the famous decree by the Tsar in which the Russian government usurped the Armenian national and ecclesiastical properties.

The Transcaucasus, with its Armenian and Georgian populations, had become a hearth for the most dangerous revolutionary elements in the entire empire, and as such it was a thorn in the eye of the government. To extinguish this hearth, the authorities concocted a hellish plot to instigate inter-national fighting that would throw illiterate and reactionary elements against those that were open-minded and freedom loving.

With the help of the Tatar feudal, the clerical classes mobilized the fanatical Muslim masses against the Armenian people, particularly the A.R.F., who had never before initiated any attacks like those in Turkish Armenia. Instead it [A.R.F.] had taken up arms to defend their centuries-old properties, which was their most elementary right.

On a beautiful day, February 6, 1905, the Tatar mob, organized and armed by the Russian police and high-level authorities, treacherously attacked the Armenian neighborhoods out of nowhere and began ruthlessly massacring the unarmed and defenseless.

The news of the barbarity instantaneously spread throughout the Transcaucasus and reached Nakhijevan, Erevan, Shushi, Zangezur, and other cities. In the meantime Turkish vandals continued their own attacks, plundering and looting and spreading death and destruction in the Armenian villages and cities in Turkey.

In the beginning the A. R. Federation was startled and powerless and appealed to no avail to the echelons of Turkish intellectuals and leaders. However, when it realized they themselves had decided to annihilate the Armenians, the A.R.F. had to resort to self-defense.

The Dashnaktsutiwn threw into the forum its best leaders, Duman, Vardan, Murad, Hamazasp, Sako, Keri, Dro, Sepuh, Arakel, Koriwn, Rashid, Khecho, Avo, Stepan Stepanian, Mkhitar, Meli, and others, and they undertook the task of arming and mobilizing the youth against an enemy that had received its orders both from St. Petersburg and Constantinople, the banner of "*Jihad*" hoisted everywhere in the name of Pan-Islam.

To organize a self-defense in Zangezur, Murad, Dro, and other prominent fighters were sent there. In many areas the Turks were the majority and were well armed, whereas the Armenian peasantry had no arms and was not trained.

We have learned about Murad's heroic resistance from Abp. Nerses Melik-Tangian,[62] who was an eyewitness to the Tatar massacres. He was the abbot of the historical Monastery of Tat'ew[63] and collaborated closely with Murad.

We already know that in the course of the horrors of Zangezur, Nerses Vardapet Melik-Tangian played a leading role in organizing the self-defense. With bravery worthy of the revolutionaries, he would mingle with the people and preach militantly to them. He would talk to the youth, highlighting

His Eminence Abp. Nerses Melik-Tangian

the importance of self-defense. Day and night he would travel from village to village, gathering the peasant youth and leading them to the leaders, Keri, Dro, Murad, Arshak, Koriwn, Rashid of Agulis and others.

Like Ghevond of Zangezur, Vardapet Nerses was a great help to Murad, who emerged from the Monastery of Tat'ew with two hundred fighters, crossed Ghapan, and liberated thirty Armenian villages from the plundering and massacring Tatar hordes.

The Russian authorities watched the bloody events with smiles and merely pretended to intervene. Instead of putting

Murad

an end to them they incited the Turkish mob and encouraged its bestiality against the Armenians.

After the horrors of Baku, the Khans of Old Nakhijevan also issued orders of massacre. Though the Armenians were in the minority in Nakhijevan, Siwnik and Artsakh, they were fearless and brave, so the Tatars approached these regions with caution.

Fear and desperation was so prevalent among the Armenians of Karabagh and Zangezur that in the early stages of the conflict they believed the Russians were the real organizers of the massacres. In their horror they prepared themselves for a battle unto death.

One night in May when the gate of the Monastery of Tat'ew was unlocked for a messenger he delivered a letter to Abbott Nerses written by the teacher in the village of Nors of Old Nakhijevan. It read:

"The Armenian population of the four nearby villages gathered in Nors are surrounded by a Turkish mob of about twenty-thousand. This mob is waiting for orders from the Nakhijevan khans to attack. The Armenians under siege do not have bread or weapons. If help does not arrive they will be killed unmercifully."

The Abbot of Tat'ew, upon receiving this letter, immediately mounted a horse and headed for Goris, the provincial capital of Zangezur, then he took the letter directly to the governor. The Georgian Avaliani then ordered about a hundred of the militia, who were Muslim Lezgin mountaineers to go with him to Nors the next day, as well as the Turkish *qazi*,[64] the religious head.

Vardapet Nerses went with them but noticed however that the governor became hesitant and indecisive and did not really know what position to take. Had he received secret orders in the meantime? Nevertheless it is a fact that Avaliani did bring with him the two clerics, Nerses Vardapet and the qazi, thinking they would preach and encourage neighboring populations to strike a peace accord and not to shed innocent blood.

They went from Goris to the Armenian villages of Sisian, whose terrified residents greeted the Governor and begged him to defend them and not leave them in the hands of the Turks who were in the meantime happy and boastful.

When Avaliani reached Nors in one day the Armenian peasantry also pleaded with him. Then, after making arrangements the Nakhijevan sub-governor and the provincial governor of Erevan returned to Goris.

But the situation got worse. Unarmed and threatened with massacre the Armenians continued to be terrified, especially after the news of the bloody conflicts in Shushi and other places.

One day when four Armenians passed through a place called Uch-Tapa [Three Hills], fifty Turks ambushed and killed them all. This was followed by massacre of forty Armenian families in the village of Minkend.

The Turks continued their raids on other remote Armenian villages, massacring the innocent and defenseless with axes, clubs, rocks, and shovels, with only a few surviving.

In those days the region of Siwnik was under the governor-general of Erevan, French Prince Napoleon. Seeing on the mountain slopes around Minkend the scattered corpses of women and children, he was horrified and shaken, and he shouted at the sub-governor Avaliani of Zangezur saying "Such barbarity cannot be tolerated and the Turks should be expelled to Siberia."

But the Russian authorities continued to stand behind the Turks and the massacres continued with their consent. The massacre of Minkend was carried out by the order and leadership of the police chief and government official, Sadegh Beg.

The Armenian peasantry of Zangezur was now in a deadly situation, with the enemy armed and enjoying the support of the government. In the meantime the roads were blocked to any arms they might get from Persia.

The Abbot of Tat'ew sent one wire after another to the Viceroy in Tbilisi and the governor in Erevan and the Russian military command, but the situation grew worse.

Here is Archbishop Nerses [Melik-Tangian's] own words, recorded by Achemian.

"One day when I was sitting in my room in Goris, gazing out the window to the street I saw a horseman with saddle bags come to an inn, then another and another. Just then a messenger from the Monastery of Tat'ew arrived and told me to leave immediately for the monastery where people had gathered and were wishing to see me, so I mounted my horse and left.

"The next day Murad of Sepastia entered the monastery from Sisian with fifty horsemen and a day later they grew to two hundred. In the meantime volunteer fighters arrived from the villages, together they left under Murad's command for Ghapan to organize the self-defense of the fifty Armenian villages of the region.

"The arrival of Murad and the hayduks, the horsemen, was so unexpected the people thought it was a dream.

"After a month the scene at Siwnik and Artsakh had changed. Now the Armenian villages were organized in self-defense, and communication between the villages resumed and the roads were opened. Now free transportation between Shushi, Evlakh, Baku, Tbilisi and other places had resumed. The Armenian population was armed in self-defense and everyone was unified with one will under one command. A smile returned to their faces. I remember when a group of one hundred warriors were heading to help a neighboring village expel a Turkish mob that numbered a thousand, the Armenian women pouring into the street with tears in their eyes. 'May we be sacrificed to you,' they said. 'Where did you come from? Where were you two months ago?'

"The A. R. Federation and its warriors took over the general command of the self-defense but the inspiring deeds of the people themselves became evident later. The Hunchaks, though small in number, also contributed with their moral and military support, and they joined the A.R.F. in the defense of Karabagh–Zangezur. Through these united and brotherly efforts Shushi, Siwnik, Nakhijevan, Meghri, and other districts were saved from annihilation.

"Then it was the Turks themselves who came to the Monastery of Tat'ew to ask for a truce, and they appealed for my intervention. They cursed their khans who were the perpetrators of the massacres, they cursed those who had instigated and agitated the two neighboring people against each other.

"One day one of the famous Turkish elders, Ildirim Beg Sultanov, came to me as was his custom, and in fluent Armenian he confessed the following which I recall verbatim:

"'May the Dashnaktsutiwn be destroyed. What a horrible organization it is to which the Armenians have submitted. I realize what we Turks and Kurds have done. The situation is extremely dire. I myself formed a Turco-Kurdish committee composed of seven members. We even collected one thousand rubles to purchase arms, which unfortunately our committee members expropriated. Now they have come to ask me for the collected funds. In the meantime Murad has been an *azhda-har* (monster). In one day he managed to drive thirty Turkish villages to the banks of the Araz [Araxes]. The Hunchaks are *bosha* [gypsy]. Ask Paramaz to quote in Persian from [poets] Saadi and Hafez to convince the *beys*[65] to live in peace and harmony with the Armenians. Our unmanly Turks will kill the messenger.'

"In this conflict others like Koriwn, Kaytsak Arakel, Dro, Rashid, Mkhitar, Stepan Stepanian, and Melik also became known for their heroic deeds."

"In regard to Murad of Sepastia, he was a vibrant and dynamic character, a popular hero in the real sense of the word. He lived in the villages in a simple and modest way. He and his followers lived like peasants. They ate yogurt, eggs, cheese, even dry bread. They were not demanding and they dealt with the people fairly. They gathered the youth in organized groups, taught them songs and with heroic stories imbued them with heroic deeds. They themselves were imbued with the highest morality. They lived in Zangezur for a long time, but never allowed themselves any immoral acts. The villagers swore in their name and marveled at their morality.

"Murad was a staunch nationalist and anti-socialist. He recalled Mihran with disgust. One day he saw on the desk of the reading room of the Monastery of Tat'ew a socialist periodical published in Tbilisi. Agitated, he turned to me and said. 'O' Vardapet have you become a socialist, too?'[66]

"He even treated the Turks fairly. He did not bother anyone. He did not bring harm to anyone, unless they provided him with a reason. He and his deputies have never initiated any fights anywhere. Their fights were always in self-defense. They resorted to preemptive measures only when the danger was great. Murad never allowed his fighters to kill Turkish women and children. He was magnanimous toward these innocent women and children of the enemy."

"The Sepastatsi was a great marksman. In the village of Mazra, hiding all day with five freedom fighters behind a cliff by the road to Nakhijevan, he fought fiercely to keep the enemy from advancing, scattering them with his skill as a sniper until they retreated.

"His fame spread throughout Zangezur to such an extent that to this day everyone recalls the marvelous hero with bows of gratitude before his glorious memory."

Let us now refer to the words of a comrade in the 1905 issue of *Droshak*:

"The village of Geomri was in danger. The Turks were getting ready to attack when Murad and his men and three scouts crossed into it. Shortly after it was surrounded by a large group of armed bandits who usurped the Armenian cattle herds. The Turkish police chief, Shakhsuar Beg himself, led his kinsmen and decided on the time and place of the attack. But Murad and his group attacked the mob with the help of the local village youth and making them flee took back the stolen cattle.

"The Armenian village of Mazra in particular was under grave danger. It was relatively more prosperous and densely populated with about a hundred homes. The Turks living in the surrounding communities continually threatened the village. They threatened to annihilate them all, men, women and children. They began their attack from the neighboring village of Shaghat and stole the cattle. However, the people of Mazra counterattacked and recovered the booty. Then came another fierce attack against Mazra and Shaghat as well. It was a major conspiracy in which the Kurdish tribes took part, led by their chieftains, Usublu, Mirzakhanlu, Amadallar, Alverdilar, Ghazakhlar, Mullah-Miaslamlu, Hajallu, Jabrayilu, and Ariklu, joined by the prominent head bandits, Murtuza Kelbalayi, Giri Oghli, Agha Asamad Oghli, Abdulazim Almurad Oghli, and others.

"They attacked Shaghat and Mazra simultaneously and drove away about 800 cattle. The fight broke out on the 25th of June. Murad came and took positions with the inexperienced youth of the villages. First, he ordered his soldiers to take out the dangerous leader, Murtuza, the most horrible of them. Murad himself took aim at him first, calling to his comrades to 'watch the white soldier.' Then from the distance he brought down Murtuza. Another volunteer Gaspar took out Murtuza's own comrade. Two other comrades of the chief bandit also fell victim to Armenian shots. Then the large Kurdish mob dispersed and fled.

"When a distress call came again from Shaghat, the boys went to help and a fierce shoot-out ensued. Murad with his battle-hardened fighters crossed behind the enemy line where the carnage took place, and the *obas*[67] of the fleeing Turks were captured by our fighters. The crazed people of Mazra opened fire against any Turk with whom they came face to face. After the brutal carnage of Minkend, where the Turkish bandits had barbarously killed Armenian women and even newly-born infants, even the Armenians were inflamed with a bloody vengeance.

This killing caused an indescribable horror among the Turkish population of the region. The echoes of this event reverberated afar and reached to the Turkish leadership in Baku, which had itself nurtured the senseless and disgusting battle between the two neighboring people who had lived together in peace for centuries."

The enemy retreated. The Armeno-Tatar war came to an end. Murad and his fighters withdrew from the battlefield. Once again their bravery and selflessness had been manifested. All Armenians expressed their gratitude. Writers glorified them. Idealistic youth surrounded them with reverence and girls showered them with flowers.

Murad's sister showed us, along other family memorabilia, a few gold and silver medals dedicated to Murad by Armenian women after the Zangezur battles. On them we read:

> *"Go, song bird, from our world...*
> *To Dear Murad"*
> *from Arax*

> *"Wherever you go,*
> *my heart will be with you*
> *as long as I live in this world."*
> *A gift to Murad from Armenuhi*

> *Let us remember the words of a poet:*
> *Helas! Combien la gloire es triste sans l'amour!*
> *(Glory is sad without love)*

* * *

The stormy days of horror were followed by a period of peace, but Murad was restless. His sword had stopped rattling, but now it was time for words to take over.

The "enemy within had to be vanquished." The A.R.F. had to be cleansed of those dangerous elements who wanted to divert the Dashnaktsutiwn's activities from its traditional path, to desert Western Armenia and the Turkish Armenians and devote themselves only to the Caucasian and Russian fronts under the banner of socialism. One of the staunchest workers for that cause was Murad.

The internal dissenters were those who had gathered around the late Levon Atabekian. For a time, in Murad's view, all of them were deserters and felons. Almost an entire generation of socialist youth who had wanted to go along with those of Western Armenia now joined the pan-Caucasian and pan-Russian forces.

We have already mentioned the Mihranian movement and the fierce struggle unleashed against it. It was 1906. The first Russian revolution was in its honeymoon. It was a time of freedom of speech. Almost everyday mass rallies were held in Tbilisi and other corners of the region. There were hot debates on strategic and tactical issues. Murad was always present in these debates and he followed the speeches of his university-educated comrades closely. Occasionally he took the floor too, clashing with his separatist comrades and verbally wrestling with smiles and jokes, trying his best to master their literary dialect by throwing in some fancy words or names here and there, e.g., Marx and Engels and quotes from their works. When we were hardly able to hold back our laughs he would stop in the middle of his speech and sit modestly in his place.

"Mikayel is laughing, I will talk again later."

Then came giggles and a commotion asking him to continue.

Armen Garo [né Garegin Pastermajian], Murad, Avetis Aharonian,
Mikayel Varandian, Sepuh, Vahagn. Geneva, 1906

So he would stand up again and smile and continue, adding his favorite opening: "Well, we lack education, we are the uneducated children of the people, so please forgive us our shortcomings."

Then after another applause he would continue with his formidable physique and handsome face and warrior's posture that are still vivid in our memory, stern and focused like a bull defending his "theses," confident and assertive and bold.

He behaved in the same manner in the Vienna World Congress of the Dashkantsutiwn.

The ideological wrestling of that night ended with the victory over both the right-wing Mihranians' and the left-wing Atabekians' divisive attempts.

But Murad became agitated. He could not find peace of mind in these constant debates. His mind was beyond the border. The Ottoman Revolution was about to begin.

Returning from Vienna he left for the Caucasus and entered the fatherland via Persia.

69

One of our leaders, Mesrop of Maku, who is at present an ordained pries, has provided us with an eye-witness account of this period:[68]

"I first met Murad in Tabriz in January 1906. It was decided that he and his comrades would enter Van to make up for the loss of those who were arrested after Davo's treachery and restore confidence among the people in the region.

"One day during a social gathering, there was a discussion about Davo's treachery, and Murad became so agitated he accused the [A.R.F.] Central Committee by name, adding that some were responsible for it and the arrests and the confiscation of the Party ammunitions that had followed it. Years of arduous efforts and depots filled with ammunition at the cost of the lives had gone to waste, he said.

"In that meeting it was decided that I would leave for the Monastery of St. Stepanos of Nakhavka in Julfa, where I would transport the arms waiting on the Russian bank of the Araxes River for Murad's group in Salmast. The next day I left for Julfa, where Garegin Nzhdeh[69] was also on a party mission. Murad gave me a letter to deliver it to Nzhdeh. I arrived in Julfa and met Nzhdeh who informed me that the weapons had already been transported to the Persian side of the border. Suren Sarukhanian, one of our comrades in Salmast, received the weapons. On the same day, Mkrtich of Moks also arrived in Salmast to transport weapons. We transported the weapons safely to Salmast and handed them over to our leader, Samson Tadevosian. Now the weapons were ready for Murad, however due to other missions he had to stay in the districts of Atrpatakan until the fall of 1908.

"I met him for the second time in late July 1908 in Khoy, when news of the declaration of the Ottoman Constitution had just broken out. On that occasion a reception had been organized at the A.R.F. Khoy committee center, where Persian and Turkish revolutionaries were invited. Murad was at the head of the table and in fluent Turkish he delivered speeches that captivated the audience, earning him boundless affection and respect. After the reception the Persian and Turkish revolutionaries embraced him and departed with tears in their eyes, his name becoming a legend for years to come.

"The news of the declaration of the Ottoman Constitution coincided with the Armenian feast of Vardavar. Murad was intoxicated with joy. Leading a group of comrades with jugs full of water they moved from one yard to another and played water games. It was a hilarious scene when the village kids attacked him with joyous screams and dumped their jugs full of water on his head and clothes. He laughed and showered them in turn and kissed them.

"Our point man from Sepastia had a great heart, pure, simple, and open to all, a true son of the people, a real hero. However I managed to enjoy his presence for only three days. Party obligations separated us and I never got to meet him again. I think he departed for the homeland in the summer of 1908.

"It has been over twelve years since his death, but I still remember him with awe and respect. He was unquestionably one of the best figures of the Dashnaktsutiwn generation of fighters."

VII

The Days of "Hürriyet"[70]

And now 1908. The Ottoman Constitution and the Itti-hadist days of the Hürriyet brought an unprecedented joy to the Turkish Empire. The Muslims and Christians were declared equal. All nationalities were recognized as free. Political prisoners were also freed. The doors of the Ottomans prisons were opened. The exiled returned home. The freedom fighters descended from the mountains and walked into the bosom of their people and engaged in free activities, at least for a while.

Murad went to Bitlis and for a short time engaged in orga-nizational and administrative tasks. The waves of the Hürriyet joy had reached there, too. Turks and Armenians embraced each other and threw joint feasts and receptions.

One day they gathered at the tomb of Aghbiwr Serob for a requiem service. Murad, Sepuh, Sargis, along with the promi-nent Turkish personalities Seyed and Hajji Bey, made speeches. Dr. E. Tuzchian has given us a brief content of the Murad's speech:

"'People of Bitlis,' he said, 'you are guilty before Serop Pasha and the revolution. When Serop and his comrades were sacrificing their lives in Nemrut, Grgur, and the lofty Sipan heights, you were indifferent. You did not even supply them bread or shells when they were hungry and lacked ammunition. Yet today you have come to pay your respects in their memory and to repent your guilt before this tomb.'

"Then the people raised funds and collected twenty-two Ottoman gold coins for the cause."

Murad left Bitlis for Tigranakert [Diarbekir] around this time, where another public relations event occurred. For the first time in many years the tongues that had been long censored now began to speak. The Ottoman Armenians too began to taste the benefits of freedom and the right to come and go as they wished.

The A.R.F. committee in distant Tigranakert had also led a popular movement. Now imbued with patriotic zeal, they prepared the people for self-defense. Armenian patriotism was no longer considered a crime in the eyes of the authorities, nor the preparations of the Armenian revolutionary organizations.

But the Ottoman revolution was still weak and the opposing forces of the Hamidians were ready to topple the new regime. They were also ready to massacre first and foremost the Armenians because their opponents, the Ittihadists,[71] had extended a brotherly hand to the Dashnaktsutiwn who had signed a treaty to defend the new regime and unite their forces.

Hovhannes Eritsian describes:

"The twenty thousand Tigranakert Armenians of the province were electrified. Our units grew in number. We constantly received requests and appeals from the villages and counties to form Dashnak cells. Vardges was with us, but he soon left for Karin in Erzurum. He had not seen his mother for many years. He missed her deeply and it was a tragedy that a few days before his arrival his mother died from shock after learning the happy news that her son was alive and on his way home.

"Our local cadres were not enough to lead the popular movement, so we wrote to Constantinople to send us one or two prominent activists.

"In 1909 Murad and Ghevond Meloyian were sent via Farzin. Two of us, Tigran Meghrikian and Tukhman Ter Poghosian, went to Farzin on horse to greet them and escort them quietly inside the walls of Tigranakert.

"From the beginning we wanted neither Armenians nor Turks to learn about the arrival of Murad in Tigranakert. It would have been to no avail. But the news leaked out and erupted in Tigranakert like a bomb. When the Turks learned about it they began whispering that the 'butcher' Murad was in the city with hundreds of fedayeen. He was after all Murad of Sasun, the hero of the Armeno-Tatar fights.

"Murad and Meloyian were hosted in the homes of Mkrtich and Harutiwn Ekanian, two prominent families who considered this a great honor. Ekanian's house turned into a place for consultations. Everybody would come to see and be inspired by Murad, and we too went with our late comrade Kirakos Hovhannesian to consult about our planned activities. I saw Murad in Ekanian's yard surrounded with a skull-capped youth from Mush and Sasun, examining his horse's hoof, since it was limping after the long and rocky journey.

"Murad asked for some powder to make some medicine for the horse's hoof. 'Why do you care, comrade Murad, about the mule's hoof?' I said 'This is the Dashnaktsutiwn's horse, and we are obliged to care for its horses,' he said.

"'Did Dashnaktsutiwn have its own horses, too?'

"'Of course, Dashnaktsutiwn is a small state with horses for its soldiers as well,' he replied.

"The people from Mush and Sasun gathered around Murad, constantly. Many of them had been with him in several battles. I remember a well-built young man from Mush waiting for many hours in the cold nights to see him. Once, after our meeting had adjourned and we were leaving, that young lad from Mush approached the Commander reverently and asked permission to speak. Murad, after a couple of questions, found out who his father and brothers were, and turning to us he said with appreciation that some time ago they had waged a good fight in their village against the *askears* [soldiers], the horsemen, and the Kurds.

"Murad appreciated the stone structures and solid homes and *chartakhs*[72] of Tigranakert, which in general overlooked the streets. 'They provide good positions for self-defense,' he said, which was another example of his strategic thinking. He barely set a foot in a new location before he began looking for such positions.

"The guests moved from Ekanian's house to our Committee house. Murad was with us every evening. We planned to strengthen our ranks with new forces and Murad visited and encouraged every cell without exception. Even if he did not say a word, his presence was sufficient to reinvigorate us.

"He visited our schools with Ghevond and encouraged the boys and girls who had been organized by our activists.

"After a week or so we organized a big public meeting at the St. Kirakos cathedral. The crowd had packed the church from the altar to the church-yard. Meloyian was the keynote speaker and his topic was The Stages of the Armenian Political Liberation.

"In his speech he said the Social Democratic Hunchak Party's activities were short-sighted and flawed and that the people had found in the Dashnaktsutiwn a growing power of the liberation movement. Then a student from the Euphrates College of Kharberd, who had been sent by the Hunchaks to organize cells in Tigranakert, disrupted the gathering and began arguing. When Comrade Meloyian tried to respond there was commotion everywhere. Suddenly Murad jumped on the stage with his lion-like mane and broad shoulders and stared with his searching eyes. Everybody quieted down and turned to him. The man who was facing them was a man of arms, the fedayee Murad, but he talked with a mild tone and the calmness of a true leader, drawing everybody's attention to the main issue, which was the Armenian liberation movement.

"The crowd applauded with hurrahs, sending a roar through the church columns.

"The youth who had first started to argue was now imbued with the spirit of the revolution and admired Murad deeply. Another fiery youth, Tigran Chakuchian, made a song for Murad. It was a militant song but with nice music. The crowd joined in singing it. This same Tigran Chakuchian was martyred in the 1915 deportations from Tigranakert.

"An unpleasant incident occurred around this time. A Turkish *leplepichi*[73] had said during the Christmas holidays that even if we stuffed the leplepis with garbage, these Armenians would definitely buy it for their New Year and put it on their Christmas tables.

"A few hot-headed Armenians, offended by this, urged everyone to boycott the leplepichis, all of whom were Turks. As the news spread it created a tension among the Armenians and the Turks. The Turks leading demagogue attributed this bold move to Murad's presence and even asked the governor to expel him from the city.

"The governor then summoned Murad to his office and politely did ask him to do so.

"Murad was already about to leave for Kharberd on an assignment. In light of this incident he considered it prudent to leave immediately. Then at dawn the next day, with the entire city asleep and his weapons tucked under his *yapunji* (overcoat), he left.

"Comrade Meloyian also left for Constantinople via Aleppo.

Barsegh Shahbaz. One of Murad's closest comrades.
Martyred in 1915

"I later saw Murad in Constantinople in 1911. There was an important meeting at the editorial offices of *Azatamart*.[74] Comrade Murad was there from Sepastia, and I from Tigranakert. Present also were the Dashnaks, Rostom, Zawarian, Aknuni, Khazhak, Zardarian, Vardges, Aharonian, Vramian, Aram, Varandian, Sepuh, Mr. and Mrs. Astikian, Shahrik, and many others, some of whom are no longer with us today.

"We attended a dinner at the house of Mr. and Mrs. Tigran and Elizabeth Astikian. Walking back to our rooms after the dinner I asked Murad where his room was and he whispered with the modesty and nobility worthy of a hero, 'The editorial offices of *Azatamart*.'

"Afterwards he left for Kharberd accompanied by Barsegh Shahbaz, one of our young functionaries who was conducting public relations in that region. He participated in the regional convention with Barsegh and visited our national institutions and then went to Mazra. In his first speech directed to the people of Kharberd, Murad concluded with the following words:

"'We have to strike the heads of the Armenian people with an iron belt until they realize the meaning of freedom. The [new Turkish] constitution should not mislead us and we must be prepared for the dangers of tomorrow.'

"These remarks reached the ears of the governor and the very next day he demanded an explanation from Shahbaz. Barsegh Shahbaz calmed the governor saying Murad's remarks pertained to the Hamidian regime."[75]

* * *

In February 1909 Murad finally arrived in Kovtun, Sepastia, his native village. What a joyous reception it was after twenty years absence. A compatriot who was an eyewitness described the scene:[76]

"When we got the news that Murad was coming people walked more than three kilometers to greet him. The meeting was very emotional. Tears of joy were pouring from everyone's eyes.

"After relaxing a bit his first question was whether we were organized. A group of us Hunchaks responded saying there was no need for a revolutionary organization, since there was a Constitution that gave us freedom and equality. Where would we to get arms anyway?

Armenak Mikayelian. One of Murad's comrades in Sepastia, who served with the rank of Sergeant in Andranik's cavalry 1917-1919

"Murad said softly that we should not be deceived by the announcements of an enemy that was centuries old, the future was still uncertain. Instead we had to take advantage of the new freedoms to solidify our ranks. 'We revolutionaries have been separated from the people,' he said, 'but we can have close contact with them. We must instill the idea of freedom in them through constant propaganda. You all know very well to what extent the centuries of tyranny have enslaved our people and to what extent our villages have been buried in illiteracy and darkness.'

"It was true, you could barely find a literate or even semi-literate person in the villages.

"Like Andranik and other warriors he did not trust the sincerity of the Ittihad proclamations. He constantly encouraged us to be prepared and to arm ourselves.

"He would give the impression of applauding the Ittihadists and their revolutionary slogans, pretending that he believed in the dawn of the 'new century'. He didn't want to give the Young Turks any reason to suspect the loyalty of the Armenians. Yet no one should take the "new Turks" for granted, particularly after the massacre in Adana.[77] No one should put Armenians into the cradles of the 'Hürriyet' because the Constitution's rosy promises.

"*'Feu de paille'*, the Patriarch Ormanian had said in response to a European journalist in regard to the Constitution, which our warriors would have echoed. *Feu de paille!* A hay fire, which would expire quickly.

"The fedayee of Kovtun, the former hot-headed young assassin of Istanbul, also had the instincts of a politician. He had tact and circumspection. He disguised his cynicism and suspicion and smiled with the ancient enemy. He made it seem that he put down his arms and devoted himself to peaceful and constructive activities. He became an activist in his native district, despite being semi-literate himself. He had been deprived of education, and yet he worshipped it. He had gone to a Father Todikian school, and he dreamed of a real school for his native village children. He was uneducated, but he had the logic of a university graduate when it came to social and educational issues. The school of life and his turbulent experiences had matured his intellect.

"'Mountains became my school,' he often said, 'and my comrades-in-arms, the Dashnaktsutiwn, my teachers.'"

The following is from G. N. Gochian's memoirs:

"One of Murad's first tasks was to organize the youth of Sepastia under the A.R.F. banner, which he did in a short time. Then he held the first general meeting in [Shabi] Karahisar. With the deputies of the Armenian villages present, the main items on the agenda were:

"a– A.R.F. Constitution and By-Laws.

"b– Education: How to promote the schools.

"c– How to keep the economic level and integrity high.

"d– Election of a sub-committee.

"He provided detailed explanations on the above four items, emphasizing the fact that under the repressive Turkish regime, all the organizational, educational and economic machinery had been neutralized.

"The deputies then invited everyone, regardless of party affiliations, to hear him speak passionately about the issues and everyone was enthusiastically in accord.

"Another of his tasks was to build a school in the village of Goch Hisar, which was completed in three months. Then a public meeting took place in its hall and people learned of his program.

"They considered him a savior. They took his words as commandments. The younger generation in particular was excited. His popularity was immense. Every time he stepped on stage, the applause was non-stop.

"'Every time he crossed the street the youth pointed at him and whispered Murad Pasha in each other's ears. They ran before him and he too turned into a kid. A sense of pride took over those kids. Overwhelmed with excitement and vigor, they would say Murad Pasha like greeting. Each one hoped that one day he would become a hero himself with arms on his shoulder.

"For us Sepastians it was as if Christ had come and the kingdom of heaven was near.

"The hayduk moved everyone with his rustic dialect. After one of his speeches over a hundred people signed up and joined the Dashnaktsutiwn.

"The Goch Hisar village of Sepastia was twenty-two miles away from the city. It was the provincial capital of the county of Hafik. It also became the organizational center of the

81

Armenian villages. A seven-member sub-committee worked hand-in-hand with the Sepastia Central Committee.

"One day when Murad had barely finished a speech a man approached him and informed him that some government officials would like to see him.

"Murad said with some hesitation, 'Let them enter.'

"The four visitors were a military major of Goch Hisar, a government treasurer, and two other officials.

"Murad greeted and invited them to take seats on the guest benches.

"The Major asked if Murad was present during the battles of the Monastery of Varag, and Murad said he was.

"The Major was a dark skin Circassian with black eyes. 'Murad Pasha,' he said, 'when I got orders from the Sublime Porte to attack the Monastery, I asked myself, why should we massacre these people, they are not thieves or bandits. I was convinced that they were fighting for their survival, but despite my feelings we had to carry out the orders of our superiors and the shelling continued against our will.'

"The major and Murad shook hands and the conversation continued in a friendly tone with battle stories. Then upon parting the major invited Murad to visit the Ittihadist Club of Goch Hisar.

"The next day Murad went with Hrand Papikian, a member of the court, Grigor Terterian, Petros Temirjian and Mkrtich Kentirian.

"At the club the Major introduced Murad to the other Turkish patrons and told them about his activities, but when they offered him coffee he said he was not accustomed to it. Then Ferid Effendi said he knew that the revolutionaries did not accept drink or food, however he shouldn't be suspicious this time. But he still refused and accompanied by officials he left.

"One day when one of our respected officials in Goch Hisar, eighty years old Harutiwn Zamanian, invited Murad to his

Murad's horse "Astghik," attended by H. Pehlivanian.

home, he said he would like to see Murad ride his horse someday before he died. Murad was startled. He didn't like showing
off his skill as a horseman. When the elderly gentleman
insisted with a shaky voice saying he would take all responsibility if something happened, Murad gave in.

"Then a large crowd gathered to see him on his horse, Astghik. I am unable to describe that scene. He put his foot in
the stirrup and jumped on Astghik who, acknowledging him
with her eyes and ears, leaped over a high wall. We all
watched in awe.

"The elderly Zamanian, cane in hand, ran forward like a
twenty year-old and embraced Astghik's beautiful head and
kissed her eyes with tears on his cheeks. Then turning to
Murad he kissed his forehead and said, 'God bless you that I
have seen this before I die. Honor be upon you, O great revolutionary.' The next day entire Goch Hisar was talking about
Murad and his horse.

"On another day, at the invitation of the Major and other high ranking Turkish military officers, Murad went to participate in target shooting with his rifle.

"A number of sergeants, lieutenants and captains had tried before him. Not one was able to hit the target. 'Murad, *oğlum, gel seni göreyim*, Murad, boy, let me see what you can do,' said the Major. The target field was an open area and beyond it the farmers' threshing floors near the Alis River. The target was placed in front of the barracks. A large Armenian-Turkish crowd had gathered. When it was Murad's turn, he took position and fired and hit the target and the Major was the first to congratulate him.

"With his rustic sweet-talking rustic manner and his exceptional talents for persuasion Murad managed in a short period to create a network of schools in the village and its vicinity. He traveled constantly between the villages and the city, lecturing on the importance of education. The connections between villages and city had been severed for a long time, but now, thanks to Murad, they were beginning to get connected again

"He also had another horse, a beautiful and fast stallion, called Pegasus, on which he soared from village to village and town to town along the Alis River, lecturing and preaching and gathering funds for schools. He helped erect new structures and had teachers brought from the city. He became an illuminator of the district and the spirit of its reawakening. He talked the villagers into making sacrifices to assist their compatriots. He even appealed to the charity of the Sepastian-Americans.

"Vahan Hambardzumian said of him, 'Murad established more than fifty schools and close to a hundred charitable institutions. Many villages such as Kovtun, Haght, Khorsana, and Kamis established schools that would become like fortresses of emancipation.'

Mkrtich' Ch'atrchian (1890-1915)
Born in Sepastia, graduated from the Aramian School in 1909.
A devoted idealist A.R.F. member. Murad appointed him as a teacher
in Kovtun. He died in 1915 near Malatya along with a group of
comrades resisting the incursions by Turkish chettehs.

"One of the most noteworthy of Murad's achievements was co-ed education. Armenian woman had been chained to illiteracy for centuries they had been like beasts of burden, neglected and subject to whims of men. To break these chains one had to send them to school, which would be a true revolution.

"Murad also tried to encourage the arts and he gathered actors and organized theatrical performances with the participation of women, both in Armenian and Turkish.

"Educating illiterate villagers was a primary goal, particularly during cold winter days, and he established classes and clubs where they would gather and talk about the issues of the day.

"The old system school did not escape his attention. The old head teachers were replaced with those of contemporary ideas and spirit. It was these new teachers who introduced physical education and dramatic arts.

85

Aram Eranosian (1887-1915)
Born in Sepastia, graduated from the Aramian School in 1904.
He served as a teacher in Sepastia (1905-1909), and in
Constantinople (1903-1913). A devoted member of the A.R.F., and a
member of the Central Committee. At the request of Murad he
served as a teacher and community organizer in Kovtun.
Martyred in early 1915 in Shabin Karahisar.

"Changing the traditions of village life was a revolutionary act. Our comrades had met many obstacles on this path. Grave political and economic conditions had led to immorality, thievery. Nepotism had turned into a serious menace. We had to struggle against this.

"The village heads, the so-called *reyizes*, had cleverly taken over many positions and handed over law enforcement to the corrupt. Murad changed this by assigning it to the young in mind and spirit. Naturally he was opposed by the *aghas*, who waged a silent struggle against him.

"Finally, he managed to mitigate the opposition of dispersed Hunchak groups. On occasions he even absorbed them in the Dashnaktsutiwn."

* * *

86

*Harutiwn Chochanian of Kovtun. A volunteer fighter from
the United States in 1915. He served in Andranik's units.
A brave fighter, he fought along Murad in 1917-1918.
He was killed with M. Tnkrian during the retreat in Eaghan.*

But Murad was not satisfied with just cultural activities. His
main goal was to organize the Armenian people and prepare
them for self-defense, even during that peaceful period
behind the veil of reform.

Like many others he had no illusion about the sincerity of
the Turkish revolution. The Adana massacre destroyed that
illusion for good. After the Adana massacre the governor of
Sivas summoned Murad and tried to exonerate him. He put
the blame on the shoulders of Sultan Hamid, then wanted to
know Murad's opinion of this. But Murad spoke clearly and
frankly. He expressed disappointment that the liberation
army had participated in the massacre. The governor tried to
excuse this and said that it was because of a misunderstand-
ing and that he hoped they could prevent further tragedies
through harmonious cooperation.

But the Turkish mob was preparing for another one. There
was no doubt that following the Adana massacre; Sepastia
would experience a similar massacre. Weapons and ammuni-

Vahan Hambardzumian, one of Murad's revolutionary disciples.

tion were being distributed in the Turkish neighborhoods. They even transported kerosene in tin containers to set the Armenian neighborhoods on fire when the attacks began.

Murad went to work immediately. He gathered his comrades, and a military body was elected, including Vardan Shahbaz. He took the map of Sepastia, color-coded the Armenian and Turkish villages, and then gave instructions to move the small Armenian clusters in the Turkish neighborhoods to the Armenian districts. Finally he planned the self-defense positions of the groups in the *Mektepi Harbiyeh* (Military Academy) and the Protestant school where the nec-

Oskan Sahakian, one of Murad's comrades

essary ammunitions and arms were to be transported. The
locations of the hidden weapons were trusted to a joint group
of representatives, two Dashnaks, two Hunchaks, and others.

In the city of Sepastia proper, in a neighborhood call Lich,
near the Turkish neighborhood, an underground weapons
depot that was dug by our comrades may have remained to
this day. At the time of the Turkish attacks, volunteers con-

Aramian School, Sepastia

cealed as Turks crossed the Turkish neighborhood and found weapons there during the fighting, causing confusion among the Turkish ranks.

The roots of the 1915 calamity went back to the massacre in Adana, but the Armenians of Sepastia would inflict a deep wound on the enemy. The Armenian secret guards watched from various positions. Murad himself made his nightly rounds from post to post.

One day there was uproar when the body of a Turk was found near the Monastery of Anapat. This was a ploy concocted by Turkish conspirators. The father of the deceased, who had relied on the Armenians and did not want to hurt them, went and testified to the authorities that his son was killed by the Turkish aghas. However, there was no shortage of pretexts to organize a massacre. The only reason that the Turks remained quiet was mainly thanks to the self-defense units and their prominent commander and the fear he caused among the Turks. The Turks saw that the Sepastians were not going to

90

The Sepastia Mother Cathedral.[78] *Centuries ago, in 1599,*
the cathedral was taken over by the Turks. It was rebuilt in 1611,
and repaired in 1705. In 1733, the building of the prelacy was
completely overhauled. Almost a century later, on June 25, 1803,
the building of 2 monasteries, 2 vestries, 7 solid altars, 5 doors,
12 columns and 24 windows commenced. The construction was
completed on September 13 of the same year.

allow themselves to be massacred as they were in 1895; instead
they were going to inflict heavy losses on their adversary.

Nevertheless, the threat of massacre remained like a recur-
ring nightmare, and the Warrior did not rest in his vigilance.

The front facade of the Turkish government building in Sepastia.
In the distance, a Turkish Major introduces Murad to the
local population as an Armenian fedayee.

The following is from an eyewitness. Tasnapetian recalls a crowded meeting "late at night" in front of the A.R.F. Club of Sivas and Murad's prophetic words:

"I do not forget those glorious days during the commemoration of the invention of the Armenian alphabet. Amid the fireworks and bon fires and the dancing and rejoicing, we honored Murad who then began preaching to us about self-defense.

"'My dear compatriots,' he said, 'if you want this glorious day to be immortalized from generation to generation, begin thinking of self-defense from this moment on. I smell worse days that are to follow this glorious one. If you do not think about this now, God protect you.'

"After Adana, the specter of pillage and plunder hung like a Damoclean sword over the Armenians of the district. Feeling helpless like those in 1895, they had become fatalistic and resigned to God's will. Witnessing this the heart of the warrior began to bleed, particularly when weapons and ammunition were lacking. Unable to fill the gap with merely his organizational skills he told the peasantry, 'what good is it if you own a stable and a few cows and bulls? Tomorrow the Turks will come and take not only your animals but also your child and then slaughter you like sheep, as they did in 1895. Isn't it better if you sold one of your bulls and bought a weapon instead?'

"Then with the patience of a kindergarten teacher he taught them the use of those weapons.

"One day he spoke in the village of Haght after the church service, and the church was filled with an audience of about two thousand who sat in stone silence.

"'Brothers and sisters,' he said, 'the most imperative things for survival of our people are arms, education, and the plough. Cattle have horns, the cat its paws, and the dog its fangs. Try to bother them and they will defend themselves with these. You must do the same with what you have.'

"Above Haght, pointing to the sky from the slopes of the mountains, was the famous St. Hreshtakapet Monastery, built in the days of Senekerim. Every year on the occasion of the Vardavar a large crowd of people from the neighboring villages gathered there in a pilgrimage. There were sacrifices, feasts, parties and sometimes also fights, which broke out among the hotheaded youth. *Zaptiyes* [Turkish police] were always present to break up these fights.

"Murad not only got rid of these fights but also kept the *zaptiyes* away and used the occasion for another of his patriotic speeches. In 1911 he spoke again about the need for arms, education and the plough. Then he turned the talk over to Bishop Torgom, the prelate and Shavarsh vardapet of Sepastia, who in turn made their own beautiful patriotic sermons.

The Bridge of Bogh Aziz, where in 1915 the Turkish officials brazened and nailed the feet of Nikol Kehian and others with horseshoes and threw them off the bridge.

"The Monastery was the *khmbapet*'s [Murad's] favorite place, and he was the shining star of the pilgrims. He intended to establish an agricultural school in that monastery.

"'Learn to defend yourselves' he kept saying. 'Sell anything you can to buy weapons.'

"Under his supervision militia groups and special units were formed to import arms from abroad. Vardan Shahbaz said he organized the entire region with the help of a just few selfless comrades who were members of the Central Committee, the pharmacist Vahan Vardanian; the physician Arshak Poghosian, Hovhannes Poladian, and Tigran Guyumjian.[79]

"In the city he not only organized the professional class but the youth and even the wealthy merchants. A woman's society was also formed. And on behalf of the central Committee Hovhannes Poladian was assigned to keep in contact with the Ittihadists.

"Murad made every effort to prevent any inter-party conflict. An opposition party was almost non-existent. However, once in a while a few individuals, to make their presence felt,

Bidza of Zmar and Vardan Shahbaz

intruded in the name of the Hunchak party. The regional functionary of the Hunchak Party, Vahagn Nalpandian, was ordered to organize and arm the population and avoid any inter-party disputes.

"Spending many sleepless nights, Murad toured the remotest villages, and after he preached to them many sold their yokes and bought arms. The Greeks who made Kra rifles that had become outdated, replaced them with Manchlers. In a short period about sixty Manchlers were brought to the region through Sasun and a large number of ten millimeter Mausers. Murad armed all the militia groups in the cities and villages with new firearms or sold them at cost to the peasants. Those on the opposition exploited the situation and turned it into an arms trade. All this transpired in 1910. Despite the constant requests of the city dwellers for Murad to settle in Sivas, he preferred insightfully to stay in the villages and not to be hampered by any city connections and thus continue his work freely. He did not trust the governor's friendliness nor the invitations from sycophantic Turks who tried to conceal their darker sides. The traps of these invitations were to become clear later."

Regarding Murad's relations with the Turks, another son of Sepastia, Mkrtich Mikayelian, wrote:

"Every time he came to our village, he stayed in our house, and because of this the local Turks were scared of me. I was Murad Pasha's friend, they said, so I must have had a grenade in my pocket. However if an Armenian had business with a Turk or the government, his connection with Murad could help him, since Murad was a friend to all kinds of government employees. He was most friendly with the Major.

"He was in contact with the organizations in Tivrik, Karahisar, and Kirin, so if necessary they could fend off the Armenian-hating mobs with a united front. He was excited with his achievements and used to say that he was confident that in the case of looting or armed attacks, Armenians could defend themselves, and this time the Turks would find them well-trained and aware of their interests."

In 1911, when he went to Constantinople as a delegate to the A.R.F. World Congress, his opponents took advantage of his long absence and maliciously spread news regarding the Women's Relief Society saying he had solicited funds in its name and then took off.

Vardan Shahbaz added the following:

"When Murad returned from Constantinople and learned about the derogatory talk about him, he met with the Women's

Society and said, 'I took all your funds and spent them. Now I have returned. Bring your books so that I can return to every one of you your money.' Then he sat and waited but no one moved."

Another compatriot, T. Korkosian, wrote from America the following heart warming memoir of him:

"Around the time of the new Ottoman constitution, the Armenian people were intoxicated with their new freedom, and different political activists and revolutionaries poured into the districts from Constantinople. It was then that I met the great soldier on the school stage of Lusaber in Sepastia.

"He looked barely forty years old, of medium height with broad shoulders, his eyes like an eagle's in a bright face with a broad chin, a moustache and a broad forehead and thick black hair, his voice coarse but impressive, his expression irresistibly attractive.

"He spoke clearly and straightforward and informally, vibrant and firm, convincing and pragmatic, mesmerizing thousands.

"In those days in Sepastia I had seen many activists who were more educated and eloquent, but to this day it is Murad's bright face which has remained etched in my heart.

"After the speech a group of boys did not let him alone. In a private room in the school we surrounded him and asked him to tell us an episode from his revolutionary life, but he calmed us down with his modesty and said he had merely been trusted with the task of taking bread and water to Andranik and Gevorg Chavush in the mountains of Sasun."

Three years later, in the autumn of 1912, I met him for the second time in Evdokia [Theodosia], where he had also capti- vated the youth. My mother had also come to Evdokia for a visit around that time, and she stayed about two months with me then had to rush back to my siblings in Sepastia. But being a woman, how was she going to travel by herself? I learned that Murad was also preparing to depart for Sepastia. Although hesitating, I asked him to take her with him. He already had two companions, he said, and that there was not room in the carriage for another person, but he assured me with pleasure that he would take my mother as his own. At the Maritza Hanum Motel on the day of the departure I bade farewell to my mother and wished Murad and his companions a happy journey with a confident heart. Four days later my brother informed me from Sepastia that my mother made it home safely. His letter, he also added the following anecdote.

"'Mother's journey from Evdokia to Sepastia with Murad has been an extremely pleasant and unforgettable experience. However on the first day stopping for lunch on the summit of Chamle Peli she forgot her silk scarf and only realized its absence after descending and arriving at the Yeni Khan. The poor woman did not want to make a big thing out of it, but the sadness in her face betrayed her. Affected by this, Murad jumped on one of the horses of the carriage, climbed the mountain and after two and a half hours of riding the torturous road found the scarf and returned late that night.'"

> *"Yuvru tghay e Murad*
> *Hazar ka mek chi arzher*
> *Mek ka hazarner karzhe"*[80]

Murad had reverence toward the elderly and the latter loved him in return.

He had his moments of rage, but in general he was warm, easy going and kind. He went to extreme lengths to bring harmony and cooperation between the Hunchaks and other adversaries of the Dashnaktsutiwn. In late 1910, Oskan Erkanian of Sepastia, who had served in the Ottoman army during the World War, said:

"One Sunday the Hunchaks and Dashnaks gathered at the home of the furrier Nshan Ter Hovhannesian. Representing the Dashnaks were Murad the chairman, Kaytsak Arakel, Vardan Shahbaz, Vahan Vardanian, Hovhannes Poladian, Harutiwn Vardukian, Vahan Metsaturian, Harutiwn Tamlamayian. From the Hunchaks were Grigor Nalbandian, Murad of Khorakhon, Mihran Chugaszian, Mihran Ispirian, Tigran Shirinian, Teve Tigran, and Stepan Tellalian.

Regarding the question of self-defense there was no disagreement. The dispute emerged about the name of the united Organization and whether it should be "The A. R. Federation and its Sister The Hunchak Party." Tigran Shirinian, Teve Tigran, and others left the meeting. Murad, disappointed by the failure of the negotiation said it was unfortunate that the Dashnaks gave in, thus conceding to the enemy. Yet still hopeful for a united front, he did not despair and continued meeting with the leaders of the opposition.

* * *

Here is our correspondent, Tasnapetian again, writing from Jerusalem about our great compatriot and his legendary Pegasus and Astghik:

"Murad had formed from the best Dashnak lads of Sepastia and its vicinity some militia groups of about a dozen who engaged in military exercises several times a week. The exercises in Sivas were held on Merekiwm mountain, about an hour and a half from the city. Every member had to fire about a dozen shells. The boys were strictly prohibited to fire unnecessarily.

"One day, in order to test the selflessness and spirit of sacrifice in the boys, Murad said, 'who among you is brave enough to stand before me holding an egg or a coffee cup on his head that I will use it as target.' Although no one doubted

Aram Tasnapetian

Murad's marksmanship, very few agreed to endanger their lives in this risky exercise, which was a sign of their fear and inexperience. There were many stories about Murad's marksmanship. Here is one that I heard from my father: A group of freedom fighters were crossing a gorge near Sasun when they encountered a tribe of Kurdish herdsmen. Murad noticed that the chieftain was aiming at them through a small opening. He immediately knelt down, aimed his musket at the Kurdish chieftain's eye through the opening and brought him down.

"During the Adana massacre, Sivas was also in horror and shock. Murad, immediately, distributed weapons to every

Armenian household in the Turkish neighborhood, and then stationed his boys in those houses that were in strategic positions. He then moved hundreds of gallons of kerosene to these places. All of this of course was done secretly.

"One Sunday, as he was preparing to speak at the national school, a Turkish captain, who had just arrived in Sivas, showed up. Having learned about Murad's lecture, he came and opening his way through the crowd toward Murad he embraced and kissed his hands and forehead with tears in his eyes. Introducing himself, he took a seat next to him. We were totally amazed and watched them in astonishment. Finally, after the panel of speakers finished their presentations, the officer asked for permission to speak and then said he had been one of the fighters against thousands of soldiers on the plain of Mush. The battle had ended with their defeat and he had fallen wounded. Murad had taken him on his shoulders to the revolutionaries' hiding place in a cave. There his wounds were treated and then Murad took him to safety. He had come to Sivas to express his gratitude.

"It must have been 1910 when the Armenakan-Abelian theatrical cast came to Sepastia. They were to stay in the A.R.F. club where they had some acquaintances. Learning about their intention to present the Valley of Tears at the national school, some Hunchaks decided to disrupt the performance by faking a fight in the next-door hall. The local Dashnak committee learned about this and Murad rushed there with his own group. The Hunchak *bashi-bozooks*,[81] butchers, ironsmiths, and rag-tags had come with shovels, and when they saw Murad they froze on the spot and quietly sneaked out without making any noise or commotion.

"Murad in the course of his stay in Sivas had had two select horses, Astghik and Pegasus. Astghik was his old friend. She had been with him from the old revolutionary days, but one day she got sick with an incurable disease and cost Murad

The Monastery of St. Nshan, Sepastia,
where Murad's wedding took place in 1910

hundreds. Having realized that there was no cure to relieve the poor animal from agony, he tied her to a tree with tears in his eyes and ordered her to be shot. He could not take the pain of the loss. She had saved him from many deadly situations. He got a new horse, which he trained from a very young age as a father nurtures and brings up a son or an officer his favorite soldier. Daniel Varuzhan named it Pegasus. He did not let anyone but Murad get near, not even with food. When ordered, he would run and stand at attention before his master, then he would not move until given an order, even if you fired a cannon. He was extremely fast, like a bird.

Once, during the early spring, a horse race was organized in the forest near the Monastery of St. Nshan.[82] I happened to be there and witnessed Pegasus' victory. The cattle herders of Davar had led their horses to the field for sheep sheering. Murad had done the same. The people of Davar, who were predominantly Hunchaks were confident in the competition with Pegasus. Murad accepted the challenge with pleasure. About ten horsemen lined up, Murad among them. The race commenced from a queue, and although Murad delayed for about three seconds on purpose, Pegasus lept like a stroke of lightning, then passed everyone and returned victorious leaving everyone astonished.

One day I came across Murad on Pegasus, accompanied by Varuzhan and Shavarsh vardapet Sahakian, the prelate of Tokat. The sun was already falling in the west and a breeze blew through the huge cedar forest near the Monastery of St. Nshan, cooling the hot summer day. Our three horsemen, like three immortal heroes, one of sword, one of pen, and the third of the cross and Bible, left the Monastery of St. Nshan and proceeded in the direction of one called Anapat, where a national orphanage was established. It was quite a scene, the march of the three Armenian figures, Murad with his formidable figure, Varuzhan with his meditating face, and the vardapet in his silk vest soaring in the wind.

"In the morning of that same day, when the entire city was preparing to go to the monastery, they had their photo taken of one of the Enkapapian brothers, the Vardapet in the center with a cross in his hand, Murad on his right with a sword in his hand, and Varuzhan on the left with his immortal pen in hand.

"Murad could also preach clearly in Turkish. One day when the devastating news of the death of Eprem reached Sivas, the local Dashnak committee organized a memorial reception in the large yard of its Club. It was a Sunday afternoon. The entire garden was filled to capacity. In addition to the hundreds of Armenians, there were Turkish dignitaries and Ittihadist leaders who had come to pay their fake respects to the great fallen hero. Presiding over the event was the Primate of Sepastia, Archbishop Torgom Gushakian, who took to the stage with tears in his eyes and spoke eloquently of the Dash-

*Shavarsh vardapet Sahakian. Born in Shapin Karahisar, from
the Monastery of Armash, and a student of Abp. Durian. Chief
Superintendent of the 11 parochial school of the city of Sepastia,
1908-1910. Locum tenens of the Archbishop in Sepastia. Prelate
of Tokat from 1910, and a close friend of Murad. martyred
on the road from Tokat to Sepastia on June 2, 1915.*

naktsutiwn. Murad was also obliged to make a speech in Turkish. Modest about his Turkish he invited a translator from the
crowd, but there was no need. 'You, noble Armenians,' he
said. 'You can close the doors and windows of your houses as
tight as you'd like. Let them even be of iron. You will see that
tomorrow from four corners of the world, tornados will bring
the spirit of Eprem and spread it around these houses. And
wherever there is an Armenian womb this spirit will give
birth to new Eprems.'"

* * *

Thanks to the propaganda and the new schools and the arms of their self-defense, the Armenians resisted looting and illegal incursions and did not let Turks or Kurds usurp their rights or their honor. Their economic condition also improved, thanks to the new unity among them. Murad had created a firm, united Armenian community, which was now conscious of its interests and deliberated on events and no longer relied on the will of God.

This naturally did not please the Turkish mob, which was used to usurping Armenian property and was now deprived of milking their cow. Complaints were beginning. "The Armenians are pressuring us, Armenians are being armed, Armenians want to be segregated form us," and so forth. Finally the governor summoned Murad and asked for explanations.

He realized that after the Adana massacres their self-defense was natural. Murad calmed the governor as much as he could, assuring him that the Armenian people had no secessionist intentions but were loyal to the new Constitutional Turkey.

* * *

Then the Balkans erupted and the Turco-Armenian relations were further strained. The Turks learned that Andranik and other Armenians were fighting along side the Bulgars against the Ottoman army. In the meantime the issue of Turkish-Armenian Reforms was put on the table by the Russians. The Catholicosal Delegation, under the presidency of Poghos Nubar Pasha, had worked fervently with the European powers for the realization of these reforms in 1912-1913.

All this was, in the eyes of the new Turkish leaders, enough reason to declare the Armenians as secessionist and anti-Turkish.

Furthermore, the Patriarch in Constantinople, the National Assembly, and all political parties were standing behind the Catholicosal Delegation, and under the auspices of Russia they were unanimously demanded reforms. This, with the urging of Russia and the approval of Germany, culminated in the appointing of the European administrators, Hoff and Westenenk,[83] over the Turkish-Armenian *vilayets*.[84]

The grinding of teeth and the voices of revenge were being heard in the Ittihadist ranks, and this would lead to the horrors of the 1915. It was during the Balkan war that Talât's great massacre was planned.[85]

Murad knew this very well and later, after surviving the hell of 1915 and arriving in Tbilisi, he said he knew Talât and the entire Ittihadist party had been planning a mass extermination since 1912. In their eyes the human and financial sacrifices were insignificant, despite the devoted service of thousands of Armenian soldiers in the Ottoman army, soldiers whose loyalty and bravery during the Balkan war was publicly commended by the Turkish military commander, Nazim Pasha.

"Armenians are traitors to the Ottoman homeland," were the words that circled through all Turkish-Armenian districts, including Sepastia. A portion of the Karin (Erzurum) army was transferred there. The governor invited Murad and his corps of volunteers to join in as the sons of the common homeland. Murad managed to avoid this, saying the tiny states of the Balkans would yield before the mighty Ottoman rule and that the Turkish army would smash them in a few weeks, so his participation was unnecessary.

The governor's real purpose however was to send Murad away from Sepastia and thus behead the Armenians of their

Daniel Varuzhan

leader. After consulting with Alayi Bey how to remove Murad from the midst, he intended to poison the hayduk by inviting him to a reception. However this proved futile. Murad once again managed to decline. The plan had been leaked to Murad by Emir Bey, who liked Murad and did not want to see him killed. Murad, thanking Emir Bey, told him to rest assured, he would not sell his life cheap. "The hand that is raised upon my head will be severed and its entire clan will be vanquished."

The famous leader however did not want to show that he trembled before the Turks and their threats. Often, along with four or five of his comrades, he took rides in the dark and dangerous neighborhoods. He trusted and counted on his wise and smart Pegasus. He was as wise as it was beautiful and Murad was so proud of him he often said he would not exchange him for all the riches of the world when wealthy Turks offered to buy him at a very high price.

One day he and his old friend Bidza from Tivrik went around the streets of Sivas and a Turkish officer politely said: "Murad Pasha, excuse me, but the road is blocked here, if you don't mind take the lower route."

In order to show he was well aware a trap had been set he continued on his route anyway. Shortly afterwards he and Bidza found themselves facing the rubble of a collapsed wall about two meters high that had blocked the road. With one command Pegasus jumped over the wall and everybody, including the Turkish officers, looked in awe.

Pegasus [86]

My fire-born stallion, Pegasus,
Behold the high mountain shimmering in the sun
Like a sapphire,
Carry me to its lofty peak.
I saddled your back with diamonds,
I threw your thunder-woven reins
And mounted you like a storm.
My whip, threaded with eternal lights,
Like a serpent whistles on your sides;
Take me over the canyons,
Over the snow
To the sun.

Up, to the heights, Pegasus,
Burying your hoofs of light
In the navels of the dragons,
Stepping over the chimera,
Fiery amethyst on your straps
You gallop, gallop fiercely
To the summit of the mountain
Victorious and high.

Pegasus, Pegasus, now that I've spread
The sails of Thought over the sea of light
And the strings of my Song, woven from your mane,
I'll sing
At dawn
The freedom of Man and enslavement of God.
My Pegasus, companion
Standing at my side,
Your mane and tail surrendered to the icy wind,
Bow your head in reverence,
Bow it, and dig it with your front leg
Into the virginal snow of these virginal heights,
Dig, Pegasus, dig, until you find
The hidden ambrosial edelweiss,
And save—along with my ideals—

The edelweiss of my Dream.
Here underneath the snow and light,
Peacefully blossom the edelweiss of dream.

They proceeded in the direction of the Monastery of St. Nshan, the seat of the primate of Sepastia, Vardapet Torgom. The primate liked Murad very much and always gave him fatherly advice to be careful and guard his life.

Murad's response was worthy of his noble and knightly character. "You are right, but what would happen to our people, if we hid and remained in self-imposed house-arrest? We must set an example with our deeds."

* * *

Let us turn now to the personal life of our comrade. He had three brothers, one sister, and one nephew. He built for them a two-story house, working himself side by side with his brothers. He was married and had one son, baptized Georg Chavush. His wife was a rare character, idealistic and brave, like him. But for Murad marriage would not keep him from what was most important to him. The following is from Tasnapetian:

"It was spring 1910. The wedding ceremony took place at the Monastery of St. Nshan with Daniel Varuzhan in attendance. During the speeches Murad also talked and said: 'By getting married, I am not resigning from my struggle. Any time my fatherland calls on me, it is its voice that I will follow, always loyal to the A. R. Federation's glorious banner.'"

His wife's name was Agapi. She had been nurtured with the spirit of a revolutionary. She taught at the Torgomian kindergarten of the Pasha Partez in a neighborhood where the Dashnaktsutiwn had established its first club. It had become both in the day and at night the meeting place for the adults in Sivas. Murad came on Sundays with his smiling face and sweet conversation, creating a warm atmosphere all around.

Agapi was an active member of the Women's Society and the Armenian Red Cross. She was always in the meetings with Murad. She was more of a doer than a speaker. Murad called her *sakavakhos* (short in speaking) which gradually turned into a pseudonym. In the beginning she was secretly in love with Murad, but she kept this concealed for a long

Murad's family. His wife Agapi, and son Gevorg.

time, as was the custom. One day, late at night, after a meeting was adjourned, Murad, who had been concerned with returning the ladies home after attending the meeting, asked Agapi in particular how she would cross the Turkish neighborhoods alone at such a late hour. She showed him a shining dagger hanging from under her overcoat. Murad from that moment on was attracted to her.

* * *

When dark clouds began to gather over Sepastia and the entire Turkish Armenia, Murad already knew of the Armenocidal decisions of the Ittihadist Congress at Thessaloniki, and he called for at least two hundred well-armed, well trained, and selfless revolutionaries who would give their lives for the fatherland.

He had them bring from Constantinople the necessary equipment to make shells and bullets. In the meantime he continued to preach fervently for unifying all forces of self-defense.

In November 1913 Muammer, the governor of Sivas, invited Murad to a gathering of the Ittihadists for the purpose of a united struggle against its foreign and domestic enemies.

Accompanying Murad were the A.R.F. Committee members, Vahan Vardanian and Hovhannes Poladian. Speeches were made in which the activities of the Ittihad were glorifed. Murad was also invited to speak. Here is a rough paraphrase of what he said:

"We are children of a free country and are of course obliged to serve our common fatherland. Unfortunately, however, it has been confirmed that the Ittihadist policies have not changed much from that of the sultans. I, like many of you, saw and heard that the liberation army had participated in the Cilician tragedy and assisted in massacring Armenians in that region. When we talk about the defense of the Ottoman fatherland, we should not discriminate among the nationalities. We should not proceed on the old path. We all know the consequences of the old sultanate. Because of it the huge Ottoman Empire was decapitated and brought to its present condition."

Obviously this speech did not sit well with the Ittihadist fanatics, after which they made a firm resolution to remove the Armenian "legend." To carry out this decision, they found a bloodthirsty criminal to whom they promised a big reward.

That person was Cherkez [Circassian] Ahmed. In order for him to carry out his task without causing an uproar among the Armenians, it was decided to kill Murad in his own house.

They took the advantage of the fact the Murad and his family hosted many travelers with open arms.

One dark night Cherkez Ahmed knocked on Murad's door and Murad's nephew, Sargis, a brave and smart lad like his uncle, replied, "Who is it?"

"It is me, Murad's friend," said Cherkez.

When the door opened he said *"ya besmellah,"* [In the name of God] and tried to pull the trigger of his pistol.

But Sargis had quickly grabbed Cherkez's hand and took the pistol from him.

The incident created a major commotion in the village. Everybody rushed to Murad' house. In the meantime Murad had gone to a town called Zara. The criminal was caught and everybody began beating him up. Finally Murad's men arrived and freed the assailant. After a long interrogation he confessed but said he was not really going to kill him. He was released, but he had been beaten so badly he died on his way to Sepastia.

The government learned about the incident of course, but in order to conceal its plot, silenced the case.

From then on the committee and the people sent words of caution to the hayduk, but he always replied like a broken record. "As long as we live in Turkey, our lives are threatened. However, this does not have to disrupt our activities." Or he said, "The Turks are barbarians, but they are not capable of organizing armed operations."

Yet he also knew how to be cautious. He chose a different path every time he went to town. For protection, one or two of his comrades always followed him.

VIII

On The Eve of the Great War

The pan-European war began and leaders of Turkey went to work feverishly in preparing for it. The Armenian calamity was drawing closer with heavy paces.

Vardan Shahbaz wrote the following:

"It was the fall of 1914. I was in our village of Tevrik when I received a telegram from Murad, which instructed me to depart immediately. When I arrived in Kovtun he was with Kaysak Arakel and Egho in the beautiful two-story house he had built next to his ancestral hut, each floor with four rooms fully furnished. Alas, who would eventually live in them?

"After relaxing a little, Murad called us to his room and made clear the danger that was threatening us. As we waited to hear what he would do about it he said there was nothing we could do without arms. Our ammunition would not be enough for even one fight. After thinking long he said. "We have to be cautious and wait for events to unfold without falling into the enemy's trap."

"The next day the three of them got on their horses to return to their villages. No one suspected that the Turkish government's plot would be directed against anyone but the Dashnaktsutiwn, so Murad would say, "Let us not be the cause

*Vardan Shahbaz, one of the seasoned Armenian revolutionaries,
and a close friend of Murad.*

for the massacre of our people. We have to wait for the events
to evolve. If the government forces us to encounter it, we will
climb the mountains and call upon others to move with us."

With the operations for war yet to start, the Turkish government declared martial law throughout the country. All
men between the ages of eighteen and forty-five were regis-
tered. Murad was called three months later when Turkey
entered the war. The hayduk requested a number of Armenian horsemen to join him, knowing this would be rejected. He
was then set free temporarily by paying a bribe. Now he
resumed his propaganda more intensely than ever. Of course
there were politicians who viewed the events differently, but
with his insight the future was completely clear. He knew that

a calamity was fast approaching the Armenians and that the Turkish government was to take the advantage of the international chaos and settle its accounts once and for all with its Armenian subjects.

He was even more convinced in late 1914 after the great Turkish assault was aborted. It is well known that around this time Enver Pasha went to the Caucasian front to organize the general assault on the Sarikamish.[87] Badly defeated and having lost a large portion of his army, he retreated in confusion and terror. It was claimed that the Armenian soldiers had a major role in his defeat, Keri's contingent, in particular. Was it true or a mere fabrication? One way or the other, the Turks continued that claim as they did when Andranik had fought in the Bulgarian ranks during the Balkan Wars.

Mikayelian writes:

"After the retreat Enver crossed through Sepastia and Muammer Pasha suggested Murad greet him. Although this would be abhorrent to our khmbapet,[88] he accepted the recommendation and he went on his horse.

"Enver came in a carriage since his car had broken down. Accompanying us was Major Zia, his Turkish friend who introduced Murad to him. Enver Pasha got out of the carriage, shook Murad's hand and his first words were that the Armenians were fighting against them.

"'Pasha,' Murad responded, 'in the same way that we Turkish Armenians must carry out our responsibility to our Ottoman fatherland, the Russian Armenians are obliged to pay their dues to the Russian government.'

"Enver replied harshly with a threat, 'Not only Russian Armenians but Turkish Armenians had volunteer corps in the battle and we have captured some as prisoners. Rest assured we will punish them harshly.'"

The Turkish general had deliberately exaggerated the importance of the Armenian volunteers as if he needed yet

Kaytsak Arakel

another pretext to punish the Armenian subjects. The persecutions began soon after, yet still no one expected that they would lead to deportations and the attempt to annihilate the entire Armenian population.

Everyone thought that the heaviest blow would fall upon the adult males, as in the past. Murad himself was convinced that the Russian army would soon enter Turkish Armenia. In order to prevent the Turkish army from committing more plunder and pillage, he diverted them by occupying the Koesa Dagh gorge. He was not concerned with the local Turkish forces but with the 35,000 soldiers stationed at Göl-Ortu

The Turks were worried that Armenian volunteers would soon capture Sepastia, and some of them like the above-mentioned Major appealed to Murad, asking for his protection in the case of danger.

The hayduk sent his family to the safety of his relatives, so that he could be more flexible and focused in the village. He gathered the party forces and explained that the first thing the Turkish government would want to do would be to round up our youth and deprive the populace of the ability to defend itself. He discouraged the local youth from joining the Turkish army by resorting to bribes or whatever, or if necessary to flee to the mountains.

Despite opposition to this he tried to explain to the elders the government's real intentions, but he continued to encounter their negative responses. He even tried to convince the Hunchaks, but they too said they did not want to become a tool in the hands of the Dashnaktsutiwn or in promoting its name.

He then met personally with the Hunchaks of Khorokhon to see what preparation they had made. The Hunchak Murad of Khorokhon responded that he did not see a great danger and advised everyone to be calm.

Murad also sent a delegation to the village of Khantsar trying to encourage the Hunchaks there not to hinder the preparations for self-defense but to join them instead, but this also proved to be of no avail.

The calamity drew closer. By February 1915 came the heart-renching news of plunder, killing and rape. A letter came to Murad from Karahisar, signed by Vahan Hiwsisian:

"We have not supplied soldiers, although the government makes strict demands. We know that they are to be executed after being conscripted, which has been confirmed by news from other places. We have seventy good weapons and various other means for self-defense. What would you advise? Our patience has reached its limit."

Murad replied:

"The situation of the entire region is similar to yours. Try to persevere. Be patient and save the lives of the youth with bribes. If the government attacks, fight to the last man and die with honor. Make sure you divide your forces into two: one in the city and one on the outskirts, so that the enemy will be caught between two fires. Cut all telephone and telegraph lines."

But there were still those like the clerics who urged collaboration. How many of them encouraged the Patriarch to tell everyone to submit their belongings to the government and endure the harassment and not resort to arms. And the poor populace would follow his advice.

The elders of Sepastia responded to one of Murad's appeals by saying the revolutionaries were the reason for the massacre and the arrests and deaths of few people did not justify their actions.

But Murad continued to warn that "the knife had reached the bone," and the massacres would soon commence with a preemptive attack from the outside.

"Tomorrow will be too late," he would say. "A people that does not have the means or the bravery to defend itself will always be subject to extermination. God forbid that riding on my Pegasus I should one day have the misfortune of seeing your corpses. You can survive only by fighting. This is my last word and testament to you."

But his words were in vain. Mkrtich sends us the following lines:

"Had the people of Sepastia accepted Murad's plan, those destined to die would have died a manly death while others would have survived and inflicted a great loss on our enemy. Sepastia and its neighboring villages would not have turned into ruins."

Murad's desperate plea was like a voice in a wilderness. Aided by the Armenian elders and the clergy and the Patriarch's sermons, the government would carry out its plan to the end. In late March 1915 three Dashnak and two Hunchak leaders were suddenly arrested and incarcerated in the Sepastia prison: Vardan Vardanian, Hovhannes Poladian, and Shirnian, and Teve Tigran and Murad of Khorokhon who had himself preached collaboration and did not want to become a tool in the hands of the Dashnaktsutiwn.

The greatest threat to the government however was the hayduk of Kovtun and they made a supreme effort to hunt him down. With this in mind, the governor Muammer mobilized all his resources.

Muammer was appointed the governor of Sepastia in 1913. He was one of the most shrewd and clever of high-ranking Ottoman officials. Well cognizant of Murad's immense popularity, he had made efforts to become friends with him and win his sympathy. A shrewd sycophant, he had used enticing words like *"gözünü sevdiğim* Murad," and Murad, pretending to be impressed, would respond in kind to this governor whose influence he had taken advantage of on so many occasions.

That fake friendship had lasted for twenty months. Murad was privileged to walk into Muammer's office any time he wished, and Muammer often greeted him by walking from his desk to the middle of the room and taking his arm and inviting the great warrior to sit next to him. He flattered him in front of the other high officials. He did all this convinced that one day Murad would either fall into a trap by his own volition or be bribed. He wanted to win the confidence of the khmbapet and carry out his armenocidal plans without sustaining any major Turkish losses. He often asked for Murad's suggestions, pretending to seek an accord between the Armenians and the Turks. This lasted until the January of 1915.

In late December 1914, one of Murad's closest associates, Vardapet Sahak Odabashian, who was being dispatched to Erzincan as a Primate, was gunned down on the road in broad daylight, his body riddled with eighteen bullets. The attack was ordered by Muammer and carried out by a six-member *chetteh* group. When Murad met the actual executioner, Muammer said:

"I am glad you came, *gözünü sevdiğim* Murad, these are delicate times. Both Turks and Armenians are agitated, and to stop the further deterioration of the situation, I will have the killers of Vardapet Sahak pursued secretly."

Murad responded, "*Çeneni sevdiğim, paşa.* If that attack was not premeditated, it would be difficult to find the perpetrators."

This was Murad's last meeting with Muammer. Thereafter, he was cautious. The governor had tried, by order of Talât, to behead the Armenian people and kill its influential leaders, but then decided not to create a greater agitation among the Armenians. So he proceeded cautiously, step by step. First he had the leaders of the youth arrested, then would come the Commander himself to whom he sent the following note:

"Dear Murad, tonight we have an extremely important meeting. Your presence is indispensable. Please rush to the meeting as soon as you receive this note."

However, without knowing of this note, our comrades had dispatched their own message to Murad an hour before, informing of the arrests and recommended he "save his head."

From that day on the hayduk dropped his disguise. "The bird flew from our hands" screamed Muammer pasha, he furiously began issuing orders right and left. "Capture and bring Murad to me dead or alive." The hero's mother herself was subjected to unspeakable tortures. When she was asked to reveal the hiding place of her son, the brave woman would respond.

"Benden ne istiyorsunuz iş te bu dağları görüyorsunuz ya iş te orda dır. Eğer canımızdan vaz gemis, üzerine gidiniz, benden ne istiyorsunuz. Why do you ask me? Do you see the mountains? He is there. If you are resigned to finding him, climb those mountains. What do you want from me?"

Soldiers and police were dispatched in various directions to hunt down the leader of the fedayees. The governor would shout:

"Muammer, Muammer, değil eğer Anadolu ülkesinden Murad sağ-sağ tutturamazsam. Kuş uçurtmam, nereye de gelmez ermenilerin Murad paş ası, Muammer, Muammer if I do not have Murad captured alive on the Anatolian soil, I won't let a bird flee, let alone the Murad pasha of the Armenians."[89]

In the meantime, by order of Muammer, general searches were ordered to find the arms depots. They began from the Khantsar village. The police brought criminals released from the jails and after all kinds of atrocities they were able to locate some. The Governor was not satisfied and ordered the searches to resume. They subjected villagers to unspeakable tortures. Finally they found the arms depots and transported them to the city loaded on carts. Witnessing that scene the Armenians lost every hope and began to despair. The will of the youth was shattered and the Turkish mob was jubilant.

IX

The *Zulum*[90] and Murad's Odyssey

One of the most tumultuous periods of our hero's life began with his escape from Sepastia and the loss of his relatives, his fighting in the mountains, and his journey to the Black Sea.

At our request, Murad himself told us the story of that legendary journey in the fall of 1915 when he arrived in Tbilisi. It was at the editorial offices of the *Horizon*. The summary of the story was published in the *Horizon*, entitled "Muradi odisakane" (Murad's Odyssey).

Murad's sister had told us about the conditions under which Murad had departed. We had also learned about it through the writings of Vardan Shahbaz, whose details were provided by Murad himself, which he had received in Erzincan in 1917. Finally Zabel Esayian[91] has collected many details and published them in a pamphlet.

* * *

It was a beautiful morning. Accompanied by a young comrade, I went to Saint Antoine, a suburb of Marseilles, where

123

Eghishe Elmasian, Murad's brother-in-law. Srbuhi, Murad's sister.
Shoghik (8), Murad (6), Astghik (4) and Genevieve (2)

many Armenian émigrés had settled temporarily, creating an Armenian neighborhood with their hands alone.

A half finished building, modest, but tasteful, stood on the slope of a beautiful hill with a breath-taking view.

The masonry work was done by the landlord, Eghishe Elmasian, who was from the Koçhisar district of Sepastia.

Amid a hive of young people, a well-built woman with large expressive eyes was surrounded by her own children.

It was Srbuhi, Murad's sister, along with her husband Eghishe. We were their guests.

Murad's sister was the only living member of the once large household of the Warrior.

She was the true measure of her brother. She even walked like him. Her children are carbon copies of Murad: Shushanik, and the young one in particular who was baptized Murad in memory of his uncle and bore such a strong resemblance to the late hayduk. One of the daughters was named Astghik, after Murad's beloved horse.

Also there were the mason's junior brother and the mason himself with his "lads and lasses." Population control did not exist under his roof, even under the harshest financial conditions.

We gathered around the table with the patriarchal family and its elders and young ones. One of them was proudly named Andranik. Some of the new-born infants were crying, and the smaller kids spoke in their Armenian dialect. It was a surreal scene and yet extremely pleasant and fulfilling for me. After many years on a foreign soil I had come upon what was like a small Armenian village, and I felt like I had come home to the bosom of a family.

After their welcoming laughter I asked about how they were living and then there was a calm. Their faces became serious and the young ones were led outside. The excitement was replaced by sighs and sobbing, for the conversation had turned to Murad.

His sister told us about the last incidents in Kovtun. She told about her brother's last farewell. And she did not forget her sacred debt. Her first words evolved around the memory of her late beloved mother with words of praise for that brave woman whom the Turks tortured because she would not reveal her son's hiding place.

"When they hit her she told them to go find him themselves. They struck her so badly she was severely injured. But she was a special woman. Only a woman like her could have given birth to a son like Murad."

Srbuhi, controlling her sadness, then described the horrors her family endured in those dark days.

"One day three policemen came looking for Murad and arrested Hrand Papikian, who was his confident and one of the wealthiest members of the Koçhisar village community, as well as a government employee. They tortured him for a long time. They nailed brazen horseshoes to his feet to make him reveal Murad's hiding place and the hidden ammunitions. The news had spread that my brother had imported explosives and intended to blow up the government buildings.

"They made the poor man walk with his swollen feet all the way to Sivas. Then they killed him."

She recalled the "old heads" were like a curse to the village, referring to these conservatives as "the modest ones" who did not pay attention to her brother's pleas to retreat to the Monastery of Hreshtakapet. It's high position would have offered resistance, but "the old heads persevered."

* * *

Neither a brush nor a pen can paint or describe the heart-wrenching farewell, which Murad gave to his relatives and loved ones on March 15, 1915, his comrades doing the same with their own families.

The Armenian warrior did not flee like a coward. He did not desert the battlefield. He fled because his ultimate goal was to help the entire population. He could engage in a partisan war from the mountains and pre-occupy the enemy, but the main responsibility of the Party was to arm the population. The enemy would constantly say that all they were looking for was Murad. "Turn Murad in and we won't touch the population." And the "old heads" of the community believed the enemy's assurances. Even many of the "new heads" believed it, including some of the party's rank and file. Who knows, maybe even

Murad was at times optimistic about the enemy's promises. Maybe even he did not fully foresee the hellish scale of Talât's plans. Perhaps he too thought at first that the Turkish government would spare the masses of the Armenian people.

Let us recall the reflections of Vardan Shahbaz, who in those horrible days when the news of the Great War erupted, gathered in Murad's house in Kovtum with Kaytsak Arakel and a couple of other comrades, trying to decide what to do.

"What was to transpire had never crossed our minds. We suspected only that the Turkish government's plot would be directed against the Dashnaktsutiwn. Murad would say, 'Let us not be responsible for another massacre.'

"There was no time for hesitation. After deliberating long and hard the hayduk decided to vanish so no one could say that he was playing with fate and had sacrificed the entire district.

"When the police first came with Muammer's warrant, he said, 'Of course, by all means, with pleasure. However now you are my guests. Let us have lunch, and we will head toward town in the evening.'

"Then he left them there and bid farewell to his family, hugging his loved ones and kissing his Gevorg Chavush for the last time, the young lad screaming as if he instinctively knew what was really happening, 'Papa, papa, where are you going?'

"He hopped on his Astghik and headed toward the dark gorges with a group of fighters."

* * *

Even the Turks had legends about him.

> *Murad dedikleri bir zara tane,*
> *Alde silahları gitti ermana*
> *Dünyada doğurmamış böyle bir ana*
> *Överim dağları, dedi Sıvaslı Murad.*[92]

This so-called Murad is a black calf;
He took arms and entered the forest;
There is no one like him born to a mother;
"I will burn the mountains," said Murad of Sivas.

Here is Murad in his own words:

"We arrived in Khorsana on the other side of the river, and among my comrades were my brother and nephew who was a brave hunter, and Egho and Nshan.

The Armenian villagers more than welcomed us knowing we were escaping from the Turks. At the Monastery of Hreshtakapet the old abbot greeted us with open arms.

"We sent a messenger to Tuzasar to inform Galust Agha, a seasoned revolutionary, and he too welcomed us. We climbed the eastern side of the Tuzasar mountain where we could fight and defend ourselves without endangering the village. There we found some draft dodgers who had built underground huts. They gave us a place to stay for about four days. It was cold and rainy. Our place was damp and humid. We spent Easter there. The Armenian villagers, pretending to be taking their cattle for grazing, brought us bread.

"A few days later the Turkish police came to Tuzasar to capture me. Watching from our hideout, we descended into a gorge in the valley. We made an oath not to surrender but to fight to the last man.

"One day we saw with our binoculars a tall thin Kurdish-looking woman approaching our way. We thought she was a spy. After questioning her some of us were suspicious and wanted to kill her but we said no. 'Perhaps she has fled like us,' I said. That evening taking the same path as hers we went to Ushgenam, a place of archeological sites and many caves. The cold was unbearable, especially when we sat still. Only Egho among us could endure the cold. He had with him twelve tins of vodka, and he drank from them constantly and kept us preoccupied with his proverbs and jokes.

"Shortly after we were hosted in the village of Kavra. I received a letter from my wife, which read: 'Do not think about me at all. I will kill myself before allowing myself to be captured. Please write to the pharmacist to provide me with some poison.' I ordered Mkrtich to carry out my wife's request. Later I learned that the pharmacist had refused."

Then the hayduk was suddenly stricken by typhoid fever, which he had had caught in the village. Came the endless shivers and hallucinations, and he was carried from one place to another for his safety. Worried about him, some of his comrades even cried. Learning of this Dr. Hayranian sent disinfectant and medications.

One day, news came that Khorsana had been surrounded by three hundred infantry and cavalry soldiers. There was no choice but to depart. They put the sick leader on a horse and moved him up the mountain to an underground cave. It was so small one could not stand straight.

Two days later they moved him to a different location. Somehow he was able to get on his Pegasus, and with extreme difficulty they got him in agony to the banks of the river. The river was raging and he shivered in the cold water. Even his horse was frightened to cross the river, but they had to. The sick commander mustered all his strength and shouted, "Pegasus, *kez ghurban*, Pegasus, my soul is in your care," and Pegasus jumped into the water.

They arrived in Kavra and from there went to Sakhar and then to other places, his men constantly moving and hiding him, worrying that he would collapse at any moment. He remained silent.

They went from the mountains to the stables in the village of Khantsar and then back to the mountains so not to endanger it. There was snow everywhere and a cold and fierce wind. They all were hungry and so were their horses.

Finally they had to leave their horses because they attracted attention and the sick Murad bade a heart-wrenching farewell to Pegasus who had served him so loyally and saved his life so many times. He kissed Pegasus for the last time and released him.

They mounted him on a mule that replaced the famous horse and they returned to the mountain caves where he began to recover.

Shortly after news came from the city that the government has become convinced he had left the Vilyaet of Sivas, and they ceased to pursue him. The news brought them relief.

But then came more disturbing news, which dampened their mood. In Constantinople there were mass arrests of Armenian intellectuals and in some districts large scale atrocities had been committed. It was the beginning of the end.

Then new scenes emerged before their horrified eyes. It was June by now, the bloody June of the Armenian horrors. On the main roads and by-ways there were one after another of the caravans of the uprooted, and all they could do was watch helplessly from their hideouts.

Then suddenly appeared a caravan from Kovtun!

"I saw from the summit of the mountain a caravan of five hundred people. I thought they were Turkish refugees returning from the Russian border. I alerted the boys and they informed me they were from our own village. A terrible shiver came upon me. The boys told me they had even recognized the cattle. Suddenly a great scream came from that direction and we immediately descended to about a hundred feet of the crowd. After the screams only a few were talking and sobbing. Wanting to know what had happened we sent the Melik, but it became impossible to get any news because the police had formed a tight circle."

Vardan Shahbaz adds the following in his memoirs:

"Sitting on the slope of the mountain, binoculars in his hands, Murad spotted his wife carrying his son on her back.

"In fierce outrage we asked whether we should attack or not? Vardan and Armenak had also seen their children in the caravan, but they said, 'If we attack they will kill all of them.' They had seen two of my own relatives, but they did not tell me of this at the time.

"We calmed down and waited until the next morning. At dawn we took to the mountain again. The caravan departed. We sat down and talked. The government had said they wanted to transport civilians to safer locations, but was this the real reason behind that relocation? We assigned informants to collect intelligence and they followed the caravan to Telik Tash. The next day I learned that my mother was also in the caravan, dressed in black, alone, proud, unwavering and unshaken, walking in front. My heart ripped in pieces.

"The next day a second group of the people crossed that cursed road. On the third day the remaining portion, among them the "old heads" that had believed their hearths would remain safe after others were destroyed.

"On another day the caravan of Maragha was set to leave and we saw through the binoculars that Armenians were divided in groups and surrounded by the police and then taken to the city where they were killed.

"That night I descended to the main road. There was a man lying on the side of the road near death and I approached him. It was Arakel Eartemian, a soldier of the Turkish army of Maragha. I stayed with him for a little time, pondering what to do.

"'Arakel,' I said, 'ghurban kez, let me die for you, we are going to take you with us.'

"He could barely respond. 'My sons, my sons,' he murmured, and he closed his eyes and died. We gathered around him. Everybody was crying. Our hearts bled. His death affected us all. We couldn't stop crying.

"We buried him and left in silence.

"On June 20 we were sitting in the brush by the ruins of an ancient fortress in the northern part of the Techer, listening to the roar of cannons, suddenly rejoicing that maybe the Russians were approaching. Alas, we learned soon after that the Germans had captured Warsaw and the Turks were celebrating the occasion.

"Then came another caravan from Sivas and we sent men to talk with them and they returned with some encouraging news.

"They were told not to worry but to stay firm, the Americans were going to file appeals and we would be able to return soon.

"Our guilt was unbearable. We felt like traitors because we didn't lend a helping hand. Unable to bear this we left that evening. At dawn we arrived in Eşek Siirt. From there too we saw the deported masses in unending lines heading up the road. All the villages in the region had been emptied of Armenians.

"We sent some of our boys to a village for some bread, but they were looted by Kurds on their way back. Egho was outraged and gave orders to kill the looters. The sun had set. I was against such a move. We had stayed back and allowed the massacre of an entire people and now we were going to kill a couple of bread thieves?

"Eventually we managed to get some bread. Hunger was taking its toll on each of us. On the Sunday of Vardavar we ate wild grass. We were in a very beautiful place and a sea of colorful flowers had blossomed, but our hearts were in mourning. We constantly monitored with our binoculars the roads where the uprooted were passing in a cloud of dust, the huddled masses from Samson, Marsovan, Tokat, Caesarea and Kirason. Their misery was indescribable."

Trying to decide what route to take, the comrades recommended the one to Tivrik and from there to Kharberd and Mush and the border. Murad was against this. There was no bread. No central command. The entire population had been uprooted and deported. Only the naked mountains had been left behind. The comrades knew that Vardan Shahbaz and his men had climbed to the mountain, but they had no way of finding them.

The route to Kharberd would lead to annihilation. In Murad's opinion there were only two options: one the direction of Karahisar-Baberd-Olti, and the other from Habesh to Ordu to Batum. He preferred the second route. His comrades disagreed. The prospect of crossing the sea unsettled them. But Murad kept insisting and the others finally conceded.

On August 7 they headed toward the sea. A new tragedy was about to unfold. The path was unfamiliar and they were out of touch with the command. In the morning they climbed a high point and watched with binoculars and decided how to proceed toward the East. They traveled only at night and arrived in about six days at the outskirts of the Circassian village of Kiwleuk. They had no food. Hiding behind the boulders, they saw two armed horsemen crossing a nearby gorge. They, dressed in Turkish uniforms, blocked the entrance to the gorge and captured the horsemen. Interrogating them they learned that they were the horsemen of Rushdi Bey who had escaped the fights of Olti. They were told about the massacres of Armenians in Derjan, Erzincan and the horsemen's part in them. The horsemen hoped that these stories would help mitigate their situation, because they thought they had been taken by Turkish police. The comrades killed them, took their weapons and food and continued on. Some Greek comrades recommended the route to Samson instead of Ordu and two Greeks came along. Two comrades, Vardan and Armenak Mikayelian, caught typhus, which made the journey very difficult. Fortunately they passed through Greek villages where they were hosted and helped.

The condition of the sick worsened and greatly affected their movement. But they had no choice and had to get to the sea as soon as possible, since the police were looking for them by now. Vardan was completely exhausted and he was entrusted to the Greeks until he could recuperate.

Finally they were an hour from the sea. But now they had to find ferries and sympathetic sailors. Batum was quite a distance away. But the Greek comrade, Vasil found two sailors who would help.

"In the meantime," Murad writes, "we cultivated new ties with the Greek and found provisions. But our eyes were glued to the sea while we waited for a ship.

"We sent some boys to a Turkish coffeehouse who grabbed two bags of flour, a mattress, and two tanks of kerosene. But the boys did not kill the owner and he shouted for help after they left.

"'*Giavoors*, infidels! Help! Help!'

"Fortunately we were hiding in a forest and could not be found.

"Our eyes were fixed on the sea. Suddenly a ferry appeared on the horizon and we rushed to capture it. Every moment was crucial. Either we fled or would die. Five of us ran toward the shore and climbed aboard without alerting the Turkish sailor on watch. The others came gradually. We were divided into four groups. The first one was to surround the boat, the second the guard-post, the third to watch for the enemy, and the fourth to load the food and water supply. Everything had to be carried out with absolute precision, and it went according to schedule.

"The sailors had not been awakened by the screams of the coffeehouse owner, and we captured and tied six of them. They thought us to be Turkish chettehs and were extremely scared.

Pretending to be Turkish officers we told them they were carrying refugees and had to take us with them to Samson.

"They insisted they were not at fault. The guards at the checkpoint had woken up, but they did not move. The two hundred travelers and carriage-men were also not moving. Everybody was watching us. Nobody dared to make a noise, as if they had frozen in a magical spell or were perhaps stunned by our boldness. They really thought we were Turks.

"We brought on board five bags of flour both for food and barricades should we need them. The sea was choppy. We left at nine at night. We had taken refuge in that ship and trusted our fate to it. In it were thirteen Armenians, nine Greeks, and four Turks who were the ship crew. My comrades were Egho, Nshan Muradian, Armenak Mikayelian, Oskehan Mikayelian, Vardan Srapian, Nshan Pilavian, Melik Asarian, A. Pehlivanian, Nshan Panosian and his brother, Hovnan, and Toros Karaoghlanian.

"We watched the Turkish sailors who were now our prisoners. The command of the ship was in the hands of the Greeks. But they were inexperienced and they proceeded slowly, which made the voyage very choppy. Everyone got seasick except me and two of the Greeks. Even the captain got sick. Had we become seasick too, we would have been unable to watch the Turks.

"The Turkish owner of the ship, Ali Reyiz, approached me. He was about sixty years old and a former captain of an armored vehicle.

"'Where would you like to go?' he asked me. It made him sick to see the treachery of the Greeks. 'Please give me orders where would you like to go, I will take you.'

"'We are chettehs,' I said, 'We are headed to Trabzon to take part in the battles near the Khopa border.'

"He nodded. It was clear he did not believe us, but pretending to he said all right.

Egho of Zmar. Martyred in October 1915 on the Black Sea.

"When the Greek Triantafil got seasick and lost control he screamed, *'Banayanu, Banayanu!* Holy Mother of God!'

"By now the Turks were convinced we were not Muslims and Ali Reyiz asked me to issue an order so he could take over the ship. The sailors were incompetent, he said, a one hour voyage would take them five hours.

"I said to let us off near Kirason, it does not matter how long it takes. I was tired and laid down.

"It was night when we approached the Samson hospital. One of the Turks had gone overboard, probably trying to get the authorities. I was awakened. It was bright moonlit night. We could see in the waves the Turk swimming toward shore. We fired at him and he disappeared in the water. I told Ali Reyiz to take the wheel but be careful to navigate away from the shore.

"I sat next to him and watched. The old man was heart-broken about the death of his son.

"Suddenly the wind stopped blowing. We began rowing in turns. Nearing Kerason, Ali Reyiz recommended going ashore for bread and water, but I said no.

"We became tired of rowing. The wind was uncooperative and the elderly Ali Reyiz continued to concoct plots to draw us to the shore, until I spoke to him harshly and said he should take us to Trabzon without any more comments.

"A strong wind came with high waves and we had to lower the masts. Everybody began to shout that we were going to sink. A feeling of desperation overcame them.

"We were going to continue, I said and I didn't want to hear anything more about going ashore. Realizing there was no way out, Reyiz complied. Shortly after the wind again picked up in a favorable direction and we opened the masts. The high waves kept pounding, but Reyiz was very skillful and he navigated the ship without sinking. We had conquered the sea.

"We arrived in Trabzon around five in the evening. Reyiz again tried to drag us closer to the shore. I insisted again to stay away from it. Desperate, he turned to me and said, 'Tell me what this is all about for God's sake.'

"'Ali Reyiz,' I said, 'All you have to do is follow our instructions and you will be rewarded for your services.'

"We distributed money among the Turkish sailors and gave Reyiz twenty golds. Encouraged by this, the Turks continued working vigorously."

But fate would continue to play with our warrior from Sepastia, and his odyssey would reach one of its most dramatic points in the stormy waves of the Black Sea.

Despite Murad's threats, the Turkish captain of the ship continued to weave his plots against those he realized now were Armenians and Greeks. Arriving in Surmene he again tried to assure them that they were close to the Russian shore and again navigated the ship in that direction.

Suddenly the comrades who were standing beside him noticed two motorboats, and they saw that he was guiding the ferry toward them. Murad warned him again.

"Do you want to entrap us?"

"No," Reyiz said. "They are Russian boats."

But they saw through the binoculars that they were Turkish boats and they prepared their rifles and waited. Their Turkish prisoners were scared to death and beseeched them, "For the love of God, let us surrender or they will sink us."

Murad cautioned them to keep silent and follow his instructions or he would execute them on the spot.

The Turkish ships passed on both the right and left sides of the ferry and commenced firing.

Here is Murad again on what followed:

"The sea was calm, and the ship did not move. We told the Turkish sailors to hide and we returned the enemy fire. It was a deadly fight that lasted about an hour with the motorboats on each side of us. Our shots were so accurate that six of their sailors fell immediately and hung over the rails. They began to flee when they came face to face with Egho's positions, and some of our boys said 'Ladies, where are you running away, this is a circle of men. Come, let's fight, you who had confronted only unarmed women and children.'

"Then Egho was wounded. We attended to him as best we could but he had lost his ability to speak and he died two hours later. Egho was my right arm. We wrapped his body in a shroud and put it aside during the fighting. Our mourning would have to wait.

"There was a mild breeze and the ship advanced calmly. Ali Reyiz made yet another attempt to bring us closer to shore. The motorboats continued to appear and vanish. Reyiz would continue to say we were approaching the Russian shores, but

Murad's comrades freed in 1915.

we no longer believed him. Then came the time when he was not lying.

"But now there was a new surprise. A fierce wind came from the East and began to push the ship back.

"We turned the sails and rowed. The mountainous waves slammed the sides of the ship and after twenty-four hours we noticed we were still in the same spot. Reyiz begged and cried and beseeched us to sail toward shore. 'This is the Chorokh's wind,' he said, 'we will not survive these waves. Even large steamboats can barely make it through this wind.'

"But we insisted we head in the opposite direction. We suspected he wanted to turn the ferry around and return in the direction of Turkey and this turned out to be true. The wind blew from the rear. As peasants we knew from the stars our true direction and when we noticed that Reyiz had turned the ship around, we made him reverse the course.

"Finally we noticed the fortress of Batumi and approached the shore raising a white flag with a black cross on it, the symbol of Armenians in mourning. The Russians threw their ropes and we walked on the shore as they asked who we were and we told them we were Armenians and Greeks.

"They asked us to turn in our arms. They questioned Egho's death. They put his body in a carriage and he was buried in the Batumi cemetery.

"Not long after we came to Tbilisi."

X

From Tbilisi to Erzincan

It seemed like a dream. We did not believe our eyes when Murad entered the editorial offices of the *Horizon*. He was no longer was the Murad we knew, joyial, fresh, upbeat, humorous. The pain of loss and suffering had left a deep seal on the hayduk's face.

Where had he left his family? How had he departed from them? We dared not ask. Rumors had spread that prior to his departure from Kovtun he had killed with his own hands his wife and son so that they would not end up in the enemy's hands.

Upon his arrival Andranik sent a welcoming telegram. Sepuh could not wait and had gone to greet him in Batumi, and the two old friends would remain united thereafter.

"I cannot describe how emotional our meeting was." Sepuh wrote in his memoirs. "It was like a miracle because we had listed Murad among those who were martyred."

Murad's first questions for Sepuh were: "Where is Andranik? Where is Avo? Kaytsak Arakel, Smbat?"

The volunteer movements inspired new zeal in the refugee leader, and he immersed himself in the ranks again. Hope was revived. The Russian army captured one after another, Erzurum, Trabzon, Erzincan.

After the liberation of Erzincan, Murad rushed there with Sepuh, leaving behind in Tbilisi their sick old comrade of many years, Avo of Trabzon, who died shortly later.

Murad's first task was to organize the liberation of the Armenians of Erzincan and look for Armenian women and children in the area. Sepuh did the same in the district around his birthplace in Baberd.

Everywhere horrible scenes opened before their eyes. Armenian villages that had once flourished had been razed to the ground, not a living person left. Sepuh has in his memoirs heart-wrenching pages about his native village of Varzahan and his ancestral home that once consisted of an extended family of seventy four people, not one of whom survived. He sobbed along with the Russian officer and the housekeeper of the only home left standing. It is impossible to read his memoirs and not cry.

A new field of operations opened before the revolutionary warriors, Sepuh in Baberd and Murad in Erzincan. With the help of their search groups they rescued women and children from the hands of the Turks and Kurds. Orphans poured in from every direction. Orphanages were set up in Tbilisi and Moscow in the care of various Armenian committees.

Yet there was another responsibility weighing heavy on Murad's shoulders. He organized with Kaytsak [thunder] Arakel a fund with the motto, "One Armenian, one gold piece." Heart moving communiqués were published in the Tbilisi Armenian papers and donations began to flow toward Erzincan.

Those Armenians who were rescued were settled in their respective villages. The ruined houses were rebuilt and once again the smoke began to bellow from the chimneys. The

Vardan Shahbaz, fedayee.

fields were tilled and the Armenian people once again proved their renowned zeal for life and their perseverance.

Murad also established contacts with the Kurds of Dersim and with the help of funds rescued many lives in Kharberd and other districts. The numbers saved were in the thousands. Among them were Vardan Shahbaz and Astghik, the daughter of Avo of Trabzon.

Dr. Arshak Poghosian, one of Murad's closest comrades.

Heart-wrenching details about the massacres came from Vardan Shahbaz who in his long battle for survival had moved his camp seven times in the mountains and caves, the enemy continuously in pursuit.

Murad also had another buddy, Dr. Arshak Poghosian, who in Erzincan was the leader of the hospital-orphanage of the Society of the Russian Cities. Another was Mrs. Zaruhi of Baberd, who heroically entered the homes of Turks and rescued many abducted Armenian girls. That noble woman had sacrificed two of her own children to her fatherland. Day and night she searched the houses of the Turks and crossed to Baberd from Erzincan and continued her work there. Later, in 1918, she joined the Baberd refugees and accompanied them to Kars, Tbilisi and Armavir. She lived with the refugees and endured all kinds of deprivation.

Perhaps the most important help came from the Russian General Liakhov, who had been appointed the commanding general of the entire Erzincan front. He had come to like Murad and consulted with him regularly on all issues pertaining to the Armenians.

* * *

But another calamity was to spread its shadow on all this. In February 1917 Murad conveyed to Sepuh the sad news of Kaytsak Arakel. We had just buried Avo of Trabzon in Tbilisi and a few months later another of our most beloved figures from the Sasun elite had gone. They transported Arakel's body from Erzincan to Karin [Erzurum] for burial. He was laid to rest next to Aram Aramian (Ashot Tatul) and Eghishe Topchian.

Murad left Karin for Tbilisi where he was joined by Sepuh. Those were the days when Andranik was at the height of his rebellion against the A.R.F. and the National Bureau. At the time when the entire Armenian people were excited with building a new Armenia, he had established in Tbilisi a new paper called *Hayastan*, supported by western Armenians who voiced their views about the Turkish-Armenian and Russian-Armenian issue.

Murad and Sepuh were outraged by "Andranik's organ" in Tbilisi and the applause it received. Once again it was another example of Andranik's personal motives. Andranik did write some articles in the *Horizon*, but others were considered unsuitable for the publication. All this left a bitter impression on Murad in particular, who was just beginning to discover these aspects of Andranik's character.

As we said before, in his fedayee heart, Murad had a special place for Andranik, whom he worshipped as a senior comrade and commander, but the chasm between the former comrades of Sasun was deepening. The freedom of Turkish Armenia was dawning. The comrades were restless. Rostom's heart bled until he, the founding father of the organization, tried to advise the undisciplined commander and restore harmony.

Rostom held a meeting with Andranik, Murad and Sepuh. All four gathered at one of the editorial offices of the *Horizon*, and a passionate debate took place. It was about Andranik's paper and its separatist propaganda. Rostom argued that *Horizon*, as an organ of the Dashnaktsutiwn, provided as much space to Turkish Armenia as to Russian Armenia, therefore the paper *Hayastan* was redundant and it was unproductive to make an issue of any conflict between the two. "You are not only the hero of the Western Armenians," said the founding leader of Dashnaktsutiwn, "you are the hero of the entire Armenian people." And he added that the popularity of the warriors was aided by the efforts of the mother party.

Murad interjected with warm and thoughtful words.

"Andranik, we have been comrade-in-arms. We have always submitted to our senior comrades, who have trained and raised us both. In the name of our past, I ask you to listen to what Rostom is saying. Let's all put an end to this conflict."

Unfortunately, none of this had any effect on Andranik. He had already made up his mind to take the path of separatism and severe his decades-long ties with his comrades. He said to them,

"You are not my comrades. Our paths have been long separated."

"Andranik, this will not bring you honor," Murad continued kindly. "It will lead you to an abyss."

Sepuh interjected and referred to the unforgettably stormy days of 1906. "When the infamous Mihranian movement began, I wrote an article in *Mshak* [Worker], and *Zang* [Bell]. I called upon my comrades to stay away from the opportunist Mihran. Andranik, do you remember the letter, which you wrote me in that regard? You wrote 'Leave those issues to the men of pen. You are a man of arms and should think about yourself.' Now the time has come to turn your own words toward yourself. People cannot wear two hats at the same time. You have won the glory of the people. Now you want to be glorified in the arena of writing as well?"

Andranik, extremely upset, reiterated, "You are no longer my comrades," and he left.

A few months later the Russian army was deserting the front. To defend the front, the National Bureau decided to aid the Armenian corps under the command of General Nazarbekian and form a division under Andranik's command. The latter, however, was busy convening meetings in Tbilisi, consulting often with the British and the French military attachés without notifying the National Bureau.

Sepuh, Rouben and Vahan Papazian came to officially inform Bureau's decision to Andranik. They all gathered at the residence of Dr. Zavrian and Rouben told Andranik the following:

"The Russian soldiers are leaving the front and are returning home. It is up to us to rise up as a nation and defend the occupied borders of our fatherland. At this critical juncture, the National Bureau has decided to form a division to aid the main corps with you as its commander, of course on the condition that you submit to the higher command. The National Bureau has also decided that Sepuh and Vahan Papazian be your deputies. Therefore, effective tomorrow you can get to work, and you will have the entire Armenian press at your disposal."

Andranik replied, "First, I have to know who you are?"

Rouben, amazed, said, "Don't you know us?"

Andranik said, "Yes. I know you well, but whom do you represent? Who has authorized you. Show me your official papers."

"We didn't think you would be that meticulous," Rouben said. "If you attach so much significance to a piece of paper, we will have it for you in the morning. Now you can get to work. Draft communiqués for the conscription of the youth and establish the Division."

Andranik laughed. "Who is the National Bureau? I am already the commander. I'd rather be dead than have Vahan Papazian and Sepuh appointed my chiefs-of-staff."

Sepuh interjected, "Andranik, it seems history is repeating itself. You have taken the position that our princes used to take in ancient times when the enemy was destroying our country. Bagratunis, Artstrunis and Rshtunis also raised the issue of seniority and inferiority."

"I am not going to listen to this," Andranik said. "Sepuh, Papazian, Rouben chiefs-of-staff? Ha! O, Armenian people, God save you."

Rouben said, "Andranik, having heard your reply, I will convey it to the National Bureau."

There was a moment of silence.

Then Dr. Zavrian spoke. "Andranik, consider the wires from Murad in Erzincan. We could not respond to him, and made desperate by our silence he has appealed to Vahagn Nalbandian who just appeared before the National Bureau today.

Andraik said, "Brother, I am already a commander. You can do whatever you want."

"Ok," Zavrian said, "Ok, do not get upset. General Averianov will be looking for you tomorrow. Let's go together."

And the meeting was adjourned.

The next day the National Council was convened, presided by Avetis Aharonian. Also present were Andranik, Samson Harutiwnian, Zavrian, S. Vratsian, A. Erznkian, Rouben Ter Minasian, Vahan Papazian, and Stepan Mamikonian.

The president of the meeting, turning to Rouben, asked, "Did you convey our decision of yesterday to Andranik?"

"Yes," Rouben said, "but he already considered himself commander and did not see the need of being appointed by this body."

"Andranik, sir," said Samson Harutiwnian, "We were permitted to convey our decision to you."

"I have already began my work," Andranik said, "and I am going ahead with it."

"Andranik, sir," Stepan Mamikonian said: "You should know that those seated in this meeting represent the Armenian people and will not allow any individual to determine their fate as he pleases. Therefore you should submit to our decision."

Andranik outraged, stood up. "Yes, I know that all of you have conspired plots against me, even you, you half-wit."

"It is useless to speak anymore," Stepan Mamikonian[93] said, and he left the meeting and the session was adjourned.

Sepuh would later say the following in regard to the above episode: "It is possible that at the moments of rage one slips and errs. It is possible that I paint a dark picture that exaggerates Andranik's character, which I may might regret to this day."

However, everything he wrote is typical of Andranik and conforms to what was conveyed to us by [Awetis] Aharonian, Rouben [Ter Minasian] and Tigran Bekzadian of the National Council."

Let us reiterate that it is not with revenge that we refer to Andranik in regard to Murad, whose spirit was to inspire Armenian youth from his grave in Pere La Chaise cemetery. No, it is with sadness and deep melancholy that we record the above. We record it because that episode stirred the hearts of Murad and his comrades very deeply and because we want to shed light on those sad days.

XI

After the Russian Revolution

The Russian revolution began February 1917, but disintegration at the front began even before then. The Russian
army, fatigued and devastated after three years of incessant battles, had already begun a shameful retreat and headed
toward home.

Fate would have this coincide with the blind luck of the
Armenian people. Prior to the Bolshevik revolution the vice-
royalty was headed by the Armenian-hating Nikolai Niko-
layevich, which dealt a heavy blow to the liberation
movement of Turkish Armenia. The Russian occupied regions
of Erzurum, Trabzon, and Erzincan were filled with Tur-
cophile and Armenophobe Russian and Georgian military and
civilian high officials who constantly conspired against the
Armenians. Tigran Devoyian, one of the Armenian army officers, presently in New York, provided the following in regard
to the horrible condition under which the Hayduk of Sepastia
was called to serve, both before and after the Bolshevik revolution. Though it does not correspond in some points to other
reports, it contains some interesting details.

"I first became acquainted with Murad when he crossed the
Black Sea and arrived in Batumi.

"Three day before the capture of Erzincan. I was dispatched on behalf of the General Command of the Army from Erzurum to Erzincan to conduct the army's intelligence operations. Erzincan had a central position, it was indispensable for gathering intelligence on the Turkish forces at the front.

"The Second Russian Corps, Gol-Ortun had captured Erzincan. Its commander-in-chief was Kalitin, a Christianized Tatar, and his chief-of-staff was General Kastochkin. Naturally, General Kalitin could not forget his ethnic brethren and his turcophilia manifested itself one way or another, which included an Armenophobia. His first task upon conquest of Erzincan was to assign as head of the police force a Muslim Georgian of Turkish citizenship. As was customary, wherever these kinds of Russians were in charge they had an extensive network of Turkish spies. Even more extensive Turkish networks existed in Erzurum and Erzincan in particular.

"Immediately after the conquest of Erzincan, General Kalitin appointed a colonel, Khayir Bek, as mayor and assigned him the task of setting up the city council. Khayir Bek then selected an entire staff from the officer corps of the Turkish army and set up a network of spies.

"In every village and town in every district there were Turkish officers who sent their messengers to the Command of the Turkish armies without any hindrance.

"The Second Turkish army was positioned from the Baghdad front to the Khnus-Kale line, and the Third was from Khnus to Trabzon. I was authorized to conduct intelligence operations only on Turkish soil about Turkish forces outside the Russian occupied boundaries. The counter-intelligence operations of the Russian front were conducted by another Russian Colonel. I was not allowed under any circumstances to interfere in the operations of that entity. I continued to follow the events and dispatch sporadic reports to the Caucasian headquarters. However all my reports remained ineffective, because General Kalitin was in charge of Erzurum.

"What were the relations of Kalitin and Khayir Bek? Almost every night Khayir Bek took Turkish girls in his carriage to the aged Kalitin and brought them back in the morning. Thanks to this "intimate relationship" Khayir Bek became very powerful in the entire region of Erzincan.

"Should any Armenians escaping the massacres wander through the streets of Erzincan, Khayir Bek would have them arrested and exiled to the remotest corners of Russia.

"Murad was in Erzincan in those days. He was tearing his hair apart with rage seeing how the so-called "liberating" Russian commander handled the Armenians. He expressed his disgust to Kalitin about Khayir Bek, and looked for an occasion to put an end to this calamity.

"We established contact with the Kurdish chieftains of Dersim. We showered them with gifts and employed their services for intelligence. With the exception of the Chief Mehmed Agha of the Kghi district, who was on the side of the Turks because the Russian Cossacks had raped his wife, we were on good terms with the chieftains. Through their help, Murad managed to rescue numerous Armenians and bring them to Erzincan via Dersim. Murad actually had old connections and a familiarity with the Kurdish chieftains, which contributed significantly to the release of Armenian prisoners.

"How was this rescue accomplished? Spies were sent to the Kurds to get them and they often came back with the spies in large groups. On many occasions Kalitin had ordered the border guards to prohibit Armenians from crossing over the Russian border, but we always managed to have those orders changed by using our intelligence reports.

"We interviewed all the refugees and were abreast of the arrest of this or that Armenian. Sometimes Murad brought information himself and we had them released from jail and took them under our auspices.

"General Kalitin became dissatisfied with Khayir Bek and appointed Colonel Tsalikov, a Muslim Circassian by descent, the governor of Dersim. He also appointed Prince Patzhemukov, the former Russian deputy consul who was a Mohammedan by faith, to conduct diplomatic relations with the Kurdish chieftains of Dersim. Both were assigned to run the intelligence operations of the Corps Headquarters.

"At that time the commander of the Eighth brigade on the Kemakh front, Mustafa Vefa Bey, 'escaped' from the Turkish army and arrived in Erzincan with a letter of invitation from Khayir Bey. There Mustafa Bey pretended to be against the Ittihad government. He was then appointed by Kalitin as an assistant to Prince Patzhemukov and Colonel Tselikov, and he began running intelligence operations from a border village in the vicinity of Dersim. But in whose favor?

"Murad played a great role in uncovering these networks but we were officially powerless in taking any steps against them.

"Murad and I maintained friendly relations with Mustafa Bey, who loved wine and parties. One day when Murad had gone to Tbilisi on "vacation" Mustafa happened to be there, too. In the course of a reception Murad put a rope around Mustafa's neck and threw him in the Kura River.

"When the Russian Revolution erupted, I was appointed head of the Caucasian army headquarters counterintelligence. It was then that the details of the spy operations in the Erzincan district became evident.

"With the help of Murad and his comrades about eight hundred prominent Turks from the Erzurum and Erzincan districts were uncovered as spies and taken to the Metekh prison in Tbilisi to be interrogated. Unfortunately, however, the Tbilisi government was in the hands of the Georgians, who released them.

"A few months after the revolution, General Kalitin was replaced by Commander Liakhov of the Second Corps.

"He was the same Liakhov who had trained the Persian Cossacks in Tehran and was disarmed by Eprem [Khan] after the latter captured that city. He was said to be an Armenophobe but when he saw the demoralization of the Russian army during the Revolution he asked Murad and me with tears in his eyes if the Armenians could help him maintain the front.

"At that time the headquarters of the Caucasian army was stationed in Erzurum. The military commander was the former commander of the Third Russian Army, General Odishelidze. He was Georgian by descent and he had just been transferred from the German front. He was under suspicion there. I was cautioned to be careful with him and to secretly follow his moves.

"The Russians were beginning to depart from Erzurum then and we managed to intercept a letter from Odishelidze addressed to Vehib Pasha, who was the commander of the Third Turkish Army. In that letter Odishelidze mentioned that his sister was married to a Turkish doctor who was in Sepastia. He emphasized that he was Georgian by birth and related to the Turks through marriage, and he implied in his letter that the Russians were to withdraw from Erzurum and leave large quantities of supplies and ammunition for the Turkish army.

"Under Odishelidze's command was Seyidov, the head of the Caucasian Tatar Benevolent Society of Erzurum. He also was spying for the Turks."

Thus was the environment under which the reconstruction of the Turkish Armenian provinces were planned, and Murad was right in the middle of it.

* * *

"To home" was the motto, which circulated among the Russian soldiers and officers during the revolution.

Then in October 1917 the Bolsheviks had won their victory. Millions of soldiers, excited by Lenin's calls, left the battlefield in disarray. An unprecedented tragedy was now unfolding throughout Russia which would have deadly consequences for the already agonized Armenians.

The Armenian people now had to think of how to defend themselves without any help from the outside. They had to organize their own army. In 1915 they had already given the Russian army over 150,000 soldiers who had fought and died mostly on the western, Austro-German front. Now they had to defend themselves separated by thousands of miles from their allies; before them were the Turks and in their rear the Tatars. Their neighbor to the north was the neutral yet unfriendly Georgia.

Nevertheless, even in those hellish days the Armenians, "the stepchild of world history," did not despair, despite all the conspiracies and plots.

The first Armenian republic had emerged on May 28, 1918, after great sacrifices at Sardarabad, Karakilise, Karabakh and Baku. The terrible fighting had lasted seven months, but it stopped the advance of the Turkish forces from taking the Transcaucasus.

But deprived of aid and completely isolated, the Armenians had to defend those positions that had been deserted by the Russians. It fought fearlessly and boldly until it was defeated, two months before the ceasefire, when the Turks entered Baku on September 15, 1918.

With the Russian army dissolving, the Turkish government rushed to declare the ceasefire, which they could easily break later on and then resume attacks. It was well aware of the repercussions of the Bolshevik revolution. The huge Russian army that had captured such vilayets as Van, Erzurum, Trabzon, Bitlis, and Erzincan was now vanishing and being replaced by the small Armenian army under the command of General Nazarbekian, who was assisted by the volunteer corps under the command of Andranik. The most vulnerable region was Erzincan, which was under the command of Colonel Moreli along with Murad of Sepastia and his forces.

Murad's activities in this period are detailed in a book published in Fresno, California, *Rus ew T'urk' Zinadadarĕ* [The Russo-Turkish Ceasefire] by Aram Amirkhanian, who apparently had been in Erzincan.

General Liakhov was recalled from the front despite his wishes, but before he left he wanted Armenians to take the positions that were being left vacant. Murad promised him that he would undertake the task of organizing the local forces.

As early as the next day he called a meeting of the members of the National Union and conveyed General Liakhov's wishes, and they uanimously pledged themselves to the task of self-defense.

The hayduk had at his disposal thirty brave men from Sepastia who had fought for a year and a half in the mountains of Sepastia before the cease-fire. With the local Russian officers he undertook the task of arming all Armenians capable of fighting. The National Union made an official call to the youth and men up to seventy years of age to gather at the National Diocese on December 21.

On the same day two hundred Russian Armenian soldiers who had been stationed on the Trabzon front also arrived. As soon as they learned that the Armenians of Erzincan were determined not to desert their positions, the Russian Armenian soldiers expressed their willingness to join their compatriots.

On December 3 Murad had greeted the Armenian conscripts at the Kristiniants Girls School and made the following speech.

"Compatriots, you all have heard about the ceasefire agreement signed between the Russian and Turkish armies. You also heard Mr. Arshak Jamalian's guarantees on behalf of Tbilisi. If we Armenians cannot take advantage of this momentous occasion, we will be digging our nation's grave. From today on every Armenian who is capable of carrying arms is obliged to defend the fatherland."

There was excitement everywhere. From dawn to dusk there were military exercises to train the new conscripts. There were also training sessions for the use of cannons and machine guns.

An Armenian government was established in Erzincan and Murad assumed the responsibility of the internal affairs and war ministry. From this position he sent official invitations to prominent Turks and former officials, thirty in all, including some who were responsible for the massacres. They came nervously and declared their loyalty to the newly formed administration. Murad received them with civility and made the following announcement.

"Armenians and Turks are the native sons of this country. Our ancestors have lived together for centuries. There had not been any animosity or hatred between them. The recent Turkish government created difficulties for the Armenians, however you are not responsible for this. Enver and Talât wished to annihilate the Armenians but did not succeed. We must now put that aside and deal with each other with compassion.

"As of today all Turks living here are subject to the Armenian government. Do not think our forces are not strong enough to hold those position deserted by the Russians. I recommend you show absolute loyalty."

He then ordered all the mosques opened so the Turks could continue their religious services. He promised monthly salaries for the *hojas,*[94] *muezzins,*[95] and *ulemas*[96] who used to receive salaries from their Turkish government.

The Turks approached in an orderly fashion and asked to kiss his hands. Some insisted on kissing his feet. Again and again they expressed with fake smiles their loyal submission and then departed in silence.

In an official letter written in Turkish Murad appointed Yusuf Effendi of Turkish descent as mayor and one Armenian and one Kurd as his deputies. He trusted the law enforcement entirely to Armenians. He also appointed Gevorg Chuljian to head the secret police keep and watch over those Turks and Kurds who had been accomplices in the massacres and to prohibit the escape of those Turks and Kurds who were known agitators.

Those who were known to take active part in the massacres were to be tried and if found guilty convicted to death.

Alas, Murad's dictatorship was short-lived. The foundations of the Armenian regime were shaky. It was weak in numbers and had a small army, and the surrounding masses were constantly searching for ways to plot against it. In the meantime the Turkish army was getting ready to invade.

Here is General [Gabriel] Ghorghanian about that period (late January 1918) in his detailed and compassionate study:[97]

"The Erzincan contingent was completely isolated and separated from the Erzurum castle by about a hundred and fifty kilometers. The Armenian forces carried out the articles of the ceasefire accurately, but the Turks openly violated them. On January 22, however, Vehib Pasha, the commander of the Turkish army, sent letters of complaints to the Caucasian command as if the Armenians in Erzincan were committing atrocities against the Muslim population, and the Russians replacing the Armenian brigades could hardly restore peace in the region."

"This complaint was the pretext for the Turks to recapture Erzincan. To realize its plan, the enemy once again called upon the horrible menace that had oppressed the Armenians for over forty years, a tool that had already played a pivotal role during the genocide in 1915, the Kurds. The Kurdish brigands once again began their invasions, striking us from the rear. But we repelled them and they fled leaving behind sixty-five dead."[98]

The attacks, however, did not cease. The Turks had to capture Erzincan at any cost. To realize this they had to come up with a more serious pretext. The Kurdish brigands returned with fresh forces. Our side again showed fierce resistance, but in the course of battle they had to pull back to Erzincan, because the news arrived that the Turkish army was preparing to invade. Furthermore, the local Turkish population was also going to rebel against the Armenian castle and its small army contingent. In fact, as the Turks were preparing, Vehib Pasha had already complained by telegram of so-called Armenian barbarities, thus furthering the reason for sending the Turkish army.

The army's advance commenced from Kemakh. A fierce fight ensued between the superior Turkish forces and the much smaller one of the Armenians, which had only one thousand bayonets and six cannons. The rest was dedicated to the defense of the communication lines. Resistance was hopeless. There was nothing else to do but avoid the fight as much as possible and retreat in the direction of Erzurum until reinforcements could arrive from the rear.

Amirkhanian writes of the conspiracy between the Turks and the Kurds and the deadly situation facing Murad:

"All the roads were covered with snow and traffic in the vicinity had ceased. The animosity between the Turks and Armenians grew worse. Facing the horrible situation, Murad wired a number of telegrams to Andranik and the Defense Council in Tbilisi to send military assistance to Erzincan. But it was to no avail. Murad demanded that the Turkish Armenians who had settled in Karin be sent as soon as possible to

Erzincan to give courage to the panic-stricken soldiers who were getting ready to flee. But Murad's appeal was 'a voice in the dark.' "

Meanwhile, the Kurds continued their advance toward the Armenian positions and were now attacking the guard-units of the village of Zat.

Murad sent Jepeji Sargis, the hero of Hajin, with his horsemen, as well as one hundred horsemen from the Caucasian platoon of Lt. Colonel Danielian who was under the command of Mkhitar of Kemakh.

The Kurds opened a large volley of fire at our soldiers. Two Russian Armenians and five Turkish Armenians were killed. The wounded were transported to the Moscow-Armenian Hospital of Erzincan.

The battle grew fiercer until the enemy was finally surrounded and surrendered. Their losses exceeded sixty. That victory generated a great excitement in our ranks, but it was short-lived.

Shortly after, news arrived that five hundred Kurds were getting ready to attack the guard contingent at Dzor. They cut the telephone and telegraph lines. The roads were blocked. The situation grew hopeless and the increasing power of the enemy made our soldiers desert the Erzincan front and depart for Karin.

The Armenian leaders who hoped to get the Kurds to agree to a ceasefire sent two negotiators. As it turned out two of the Aghas were already on their way to Erzincan to meet with "Murad Pasha."

Amirkhanian, who was one of the Armenian negotiators, told us the following:

"Murad, having been familiar with the Turkish and Kurdish chieftains for a long time, knew their thoughts and their ways. At his command two beautiful horse-drawn carriages were sent to the village of Meghutsik to bring them to Erzincan.

"At ten o'clock at night, led by four Armenian horsemen, Hasan and Suleyman Aghas, along with twenty Kurdish horsemen, arrived in Erzincan and were led to the official residence of the Moscow Armenian Committee before a large group of citizens.

"Commissar Baghdasarian and four Russian Armenian officers met with them and then led them to the "pasha."

"Arriving at Murad's house, they unbuttoned their overcoats and walked up the stairs to his room. They solemnly kissed his shoulders and hands and sat in the chairs offered to them.

"The Armenian leaders began to speak in an upbeat spirit, telling them about Murad's relations with prominent Kurdish leaders of Mush and other regions.

"After a tea Murad made the following speech:

"'My reason for inviting you here was to ask for peace. Do not think that our forces are insufficient, but we do not want to harm you because your good deeds have always touched us. In the past two centuries the Kurds have dealt with Armenians nobly. However, you have recently abused our friendship by attacking our guards, which has endangered our centuries-old friendship. It is our fervent desire that we live in peace and harmony and not provide a pretext for the Turks to laugh at us.'

"After two long hours of talking, Murad promised them rewards. The Kurds presented their previous demand and asked that all Armenian forces stationed on the left bank of Euphrates and in the vicinity of Dersim be withdrawn. Murad gave in and had them promise in return not to cross the river either. The Kurds thanked him dearly and left.

"The next day Murad presented each of the Aghas with a horse and a gold watch and sent them off with Sergeant Vahram Ter Manuelian.

Vahram Ter Manuelian of Chmshkatsag, martyred in 1918

"The Kurds left, but having barely crossed the bridge, were then attacked by thirty Russian Armenian soldiers on their way from Chanchik to Erzincan. Vahram Ter Manuelian interfered and tried to explain but it was futile. The soldiers ignored him and disarmed the Kurds and prepared to return them to Erzincan. Outraged when he heard of this, Murad jumped on his horse and rushed to the bridge to free the Kurds. When he admonished the Russian Armenian soldiers, they replied, 'for us, a Turk and a Kurd are the same. Cursed be the Turks and the Kurds. We are not going to release them.' But Murad finally succeeded in convincing the soldiers to release the Kurds. The Kurdish Aghas who had been shivering with fear began kissing Murad's feet and hand. They had asked to leave all their horses and weapons to the soldiers, if only their lives be spared, but they were now sent with their gifts across the bridge. One of them then said, 'This was a game concocted by Murad who wanted to have us killed at the bridge.'

"Murad, having barely returned home, received news that about three hundred armed Kurds and Turks from the villages of Btarich and Chimi had arrived and were now settled in the homes of the city *mukhtars*,[99] and a new attack seemed imminent.

"He ordered their arrest and as our soldiers were preparing to attack from their positions and arrest the traitors as several elder Kurdish aghas led by Reza Agha came to see him. He greeted them with respect and after offering them coffee asked about their purpose in coming to Erzincan.

"They were the warriors of the Memish Agha of Peregan. Having heard about the gifts granted to the Kurds of Dersim for signing the peace treaty, they had come with the same expectations!"

But Murad was not naïve in regard to the friendly relations with the Kurdish aghas. He pretended that he trusted them in order to gain time. The aghas in fact remained in the bottom of their hearts fierce enemies of the Armenians, as they themselves cynically confessed. One day in Murad's absence one of the aghas of Dersim named Pakko made a speech to the Armenians that was filled with grave accusations and threats.

The Armenians in the liberated vilayets had often expressed their feelings of rage and hatred in regard to the massacres, and on occasions they avenged the deaths of their loved one. It was because of this that Pakko agha made his speech.

"I feel sorry for you Armenians," he said. "Every time you find yourselves in difficult situations you ask for help. You are unappreciative and evil people. You are not scared of God. As soon as an occasion rises, you forget everything, including your God. You know well that for over a year and a half your honor was saved among the Kurds. Tell me, was there a single Kurd who laid his eyes on your women and girls? And now it has been barely forty days that the Russians have left Erzincan, and see what you did to the Kurds and Turks living there. Tell me, which one of you has not held a Kurdish woman or girl and taken her by force as his wife? How many Kurds did you kill by luring them to your houses and throwing them in the wells? How many children did you not trample to death under your horses hooves in the marketplace and then throw their bodies to the dogs? Armenians, these kinds of things are not going to last long. There is a God in the Heavens, and with His help you will again be subjugated by us. You will have to leave and depart from Erzincan. If Russia has promised to leave this piece of land of so-called Armenia to you, the Turks are going to leave us not only Erzincan, but also Karin, Van, and Bitlis. How is it possible for Turks and Kurds to remain slaves of their *rayyahs?*[100] If Armenians' dreams were realized, the whole of Islam would be wiped out."

Thus spoke Pakko Agha, despite the assurances of the Armenian representatives who tried to speak of harmony, while the Turkish government continued their reports of disaccord.

For thirty years the likes of Pakko Agha, in Dersim or in other places, had wanted to see the Armeno-Kurdish harmony realized, but on their terms and with them as the dominating race. Would this now be changed in the minds of the new young revolutionary Kurds? In the meantime the partisan fights continued with heavy losses on both sides, and Murad continued to struggle on the internal front against the demoralization and desertion of the soldiers.

Then came a day of mourning. To foil the Kurdish attacks, Murad, after consulting with Colonel Moreli, had sent about a thousand soldiers to the front with two cannons and four machine guns, under the command of Major Dr. Arslanian, who had been with the soldiers guarding the city. It was a heavy defeat for the Armenians. Two Russian cannoneers were killed, including Dr. Arslanian himself.

It was a nightmarish time and it became clear that under the hopeless conditions resistance could not continue without endangering the lives of the remaining population.

It is not surprising that the number of deserters grew day by day. There were both Russian Armenian and Turkish Armenian, however not all deserted because of fear or cowardice.

Here is an eyewitness account:

"We transported the bodies of Dr. Arslanian and the two cannoneers on the hearse to the courtyard of the church. The people gathered sobbing. Murad had ordered preparations for an immediate burial.

"When he returned home after the funeral he saw a gathering of about one hundred Russian Armenian soldiers who were waiting for him along with commissar Baghdasarian.

"What is up boys?" He asked.

"'Murad, brother, we are going home.'

"'There is the road. You can go.'

"'We would like to have your permission.'

"'If you are waiting for my order, I cannot grant it' he said, and he walked up to his room with the commissar. 'Let one or two of your leaders come up.'

"Two from among the soldiers walked up and told him about their condition.

"Murad in his clear and convincing way encouraged them and calmed them down, then asked them to wait a few days. 'Should we not receive help within a week, I will lead you myself along with all the refugees and leave Erzincan.'

"The soldiers stood up, apologized and departed.

"After this group had barely left, another led by a captain gathered in the square and asked for Murad who came again and said 'What do you want, boys?'

"The young captain's name was Melikian and he said that their wish was to be relieved of their duties so they could return to the Caucasus.

"Murad became emotional and said, 'May my soul be sacrificed to you, my boys, I ask that you kill me right here and walk over my body and proceed on your way.'

"His words moved them and they promised not to depart from Erzincan but to serve wherever he ordered.

"Murad took Captain Melikian to the headquarters of the central committee and after a lengthy consultation with the Russian Armenian officers decided to:

a– Add five more soldiers to guard the roads.

b– Assign twenty-four hour rotating guards in the Turkish neighborhoods of the city.

c– Transport the prisoners to a more secure and suitable buildings.

d– Prohibit absolutely the Turkish women and girls from leaving their houses in the city, since their appearance in the streets might cause commotion in the ranks and affect the discipline of the soldiers, in addition to some of them being spies and informants.

Besides this groups of ten were dispatched to fortify the checkpoints on the roads to Kamurj, Vaghaver, and Kemakh.

The Kurdish attacks subsided for a while, but barely had the calm been restored to the city when news arrived that a Turkish army unit of six thousand strong had joined with the Kurds in the direction of Pliumer and was approaching Mamakhatun.

This news was a big upset. The soldiers were overcome with panic. Murad ordered twenty of them to gather intelligence at the checkpoints. They were preparing for this when suddenly two bloody and sweaty horsemen burst into Murad's room and asked him to immediately dispatch help to Chardakhlu, since the seventy guards there had been surrounded. They said that because of heavy attacks from the Turkish front during the night, the Armenian guards had left their posts and retreated about three miles to the east.

Murad became desperate, yet he held himself together and called for five soldiers. "Boys, may my soul be sacrificed to you, prepare the horses and join me."

When people heard the commander was heading to the front, women and children ran toward him sobbing and begging him not to leave the city.

This time he could not pay heed to their cries, but as he got on his horse getting ready to leave for Chardakhlu front, there was yet another surprise. A group of soldiers came to him and demanded to make preparations for retreat. They said a delay would cause disaster. Panic-stricken people were running up and down the streets.

Shortly after, the Chardakhlu guards too, having deserted their posts, arrived and explained the situation. The Turkish army had attacked overnight with cannons and machine guns. Our forces were ambushed and had to escape to Erzincan. Desperation took over everywhere. Many refugee Armenians began looking for carts and carriages to transport their children.

Murad, consulting with commissar Baghdasarian and Dr. Poghosian, decided to plan and organize the retreat. They informed Colonel Moreli who immediately consented.

The decision was made to retreat within four days, overnight and secretly, under the protection of the soldiers. Murad ordered to blow up the bridge and set fire to all military supplies.

Upon receiving the orders for retreat, our soldiers were filled with rage and revenge and they poured into the Turkish neighborhoods and according to a compatriot eyewitness, "allowed themselves unprecedented deeds." Stores in the market were looted. Several neighborhoods were engulfed in fire. Many Turks began to flee. All the efforts to refrain the mobs remained futile.

The youth, ages twelve and thirteen, wasted thousands of rounds of shells everyday. The women cried, the children screamed. Despite the roar of the rifles of the soldiers, the looters continued their abuses and a cold terror spread everywhere.

"We have to leave as soon as possible," Murad said, "or we are all going to be killed."

The Turkish Army was approaching. The roar of the cannons was heard in the distance.

Murad dispatched twenty soldiers to Kemakh gorge to see from which direction the Turks were preparing their attack. The soldiers ran back and informed him that they were already near the cemetery.

Murad went to the upper barracks of the city and the Turks ambushed him. He ordered to blow up the bridge. The prison guards were unaware of this. People were shouting "Murad! Murad!" as they ran toward the barracks, including the elderly wrapped in rag-tag overcoats and women with their children on their backs.

Some, unable to part with their belongings, were in a state of frenzy running and screaming on their stairs. Many cursed God like the insane in a sanatorium.

The enemy fire was strengthening and the shells were falling like hail on the city. It had started to snow. Murad and Dr. Poghosian began organizing a caravan to retreat from the barracks through the newly built intersection on the northern slope of the mountain.

On January 31, the caravan began to move. The total number of refugees, including the fighters, was six thousand. Only around twenty of the sick and the old were left behind. The sick could not be moved from the hospital and the elderly said they preferred to die there rather than succumb to the cold on the road.

When Turkish army entered Erzincan the Turkish residents of the city did not come out from their houses, suspecting that after the departure of the Armenians the entire city would be razed. But when they saw the Turkish army they poured from their hiding and released the prisoners, then a mob stormed the Armenian neighborhoods and began looting and killing the remaining Armenians ruthlessly.

XII

Retreat to Erzurum

The Armenians retreating from Erzincan were losing Turkish Armenia for a second time. With the enemy pursuing them they had to avoid being surrounded by the Armenocidal packs of Vehib Pasha and the Kurdish brigands. Our small-armed units were compelled to devote all their energy to caring for the refugees while repelling the Kurdish and Turkish attacks. Many homes, and ammunition supplies were destroyed in the retreat.

Murad, as selfless and disciplined as ever, was always seen leading the battles. Vardan Shahbaz and A. Poghosian were with him. "Murad's gallant soldiers were among the last to leave the city after fighting against the massive Turkish forces," wrote General Ghorghanian.

It was like an Armenian Golgotha, and the great hayduk could not bear the cries and screams in the blizzards.

Amirhkhanian described the scene:

"It was horrible. Feet wrapped in rags, women and girls terrified and sobbing, falling and rising in the snow followed by the fighters. Small children could not even cry. Even terrified soldiers with backpacks tried to advance ahead of the refugees.

Murad, after the fateful battles of Erzincan, 1917

Very few stood gallantly with the women and children who were left behind, helping them catch up with the caravan."

When they arrived in the vicinity of the village of Btarich, the Kurds began to open fire from their positions on the mountain slopes. Our fighters took positions from the road-side and resisted fiercely. The road leading to the village of Khan was extremely dangerous. Suddenly the soldiers supporting the rear fled, saying the Turkish cavalry had begun opening fire there. There was indescribable chaos. Many over-powered by fatigue fell in the snow. After dusk the snow stopped. It was a clear and calm sky. The northerly wind began to blow. The refugees could remain in their places, yet they were beginning to freeze. Suddenly there came Murad's voice in the dark. "If there is any one among you who wants to help save lives, let him come forward."

The late Vahram Ter Manuelian, the guardian of the Dzor Breran, came forward.

"I am ready, Murad."

He was followed by Suren Aghajanian and others.

Murad turned to them, and said.

"Let me be sacrificed to your lives. We have to move quickly and see if there are any enemy positions ahead of us."

Vahram and his comrades went to check the roads. The caravan followed them. Sporadic gunfire was heard from the mountains.

The caravan moved in the direction of Chilek. The Euphrates was completely frozen.

There were one hundred and eighty Armenian fighters in the Chilek gorge under the command of Mkhitar of Kemakh. This courageous youth who fought constantly for two months held his position and kept the enemy at bay.

It was everybody's wish to rest at least for a day, but Murad refused. He followed the caravan with two cannons.

One of the lads who had been sent to the mountain to gather intelligence returned bringing news of the death of Vahram Ter Manuelian and sergeant Mruzov.

It was a heavy blow for Murad who liked Vahram a lot. Screaming wildly he stood up and said, "Boys, Vahram's fate is awaiting us all. Many of us are going to lie next to his frozen body. For the love of these kids and your sisters, take up arms and fight like real men. If you fail, we will all be condemned."

Suddenly Vahram's Arabian stallion appeared in the distance. It was returning to the caravan rider-less.

Shots were heard from the summits of the mountains of Derjan. Again there was commotion, chaos and people running in every direction. It grew worse in the dangerous gorge of Sansar. The Kurds began their attacks from the heights of Derjan. Hiding behind cliffs, they fired incessantly. They had a good view of our soldiers and killed them one after another. Shortly after another group of fifty Kurds took positions from the direction of Derjan, and a rain of shells began to fall like hail. The cries and screams of women and children stunned even the most courageous youth.

Murad ran up and down like a mountain goat giving orders and encouraging the fighters. Our positions were very precarious and the only weapons left were our cannons.

Murad had the cannons positioned and began bombarding the Kurdish positions and the caves in which they were hiding. Two Russian Armenian youths, Ter Petrosov and Ter Akobov, headed the cannons and shouted *ras, va, dree*, (one, two, three) and pulled the triggers. None of the shells missed their targets. The perfect targeting pounded the Kurdish positions and dispersed them within an hour.

The number of our dead and wounded fighters exceeded seventy. The wounded begged not to be left behind in the hands of the enemy. Many crawled on the ground and begged, "Kill us." There was not anyone who did not worry about his fate.

The caravan came across Vahram's frozen body at the side of the road. The Kurds had mutilated his face with bayonets and looted his cloths.

They reached Chors at night. There were a few wooden framed barracks that had been built by the Russian soldiers. It was a checkpoint where there were one hundred Armenian soldiers and twenty days worth of provisions, which they had managed to gather after numerous clashes with the local Kurds.

People crammed into the barracks. They spent the night in absolute darkness. At dawn the Kurds commenced a fierce barrage of gunfire. There were more fatalities. Our losses were huge. On the Vzhan Bridge in particular there were

*Martiros T'nkrian of Kovtun. A volunteer fighter from America in
1915, he fought in General Andranik's units and was a comrade-
in-arms of Murad in 1917-1918. Heroically fought in the battle
of Sansar Dere and many other battles. Martyred during the
destruction of the ammunition depot of Eaghan.*

about five hundred dead. In addition to this about three hundred people suffered frostbite of the hands and feet, most of
who died shortly after in the hospitals of Karin, Sarikamish,
Alexandropol and Tbilisi.

The caravan finally arrived in Karin. Murad had already
learned by radio that Sepuh too had retreated from Baberd
and arrived in Ackale.

The two comrades who had been separated months before
in Tbilisi met again. In the course of their emotional reunion,
after living through the horror, Sepuh asked his old comrade

to describe his own. Murad replied by commending the bravery of his "lion cubs."

"What can I say, Sepuh, here they are. If I were an historian I would bestow upon them the highest honor. They are our foundation and our anchor. If it is true that a soldier without a commander is nothing, then the opposite is true, too."

Murad liked to philosophize. But Sepuh was more interested in details and repeated his question. Murad replied:

"There were many fights and losses. Oh, that Chilek gorge. Many valiant fighters were lost there. Our suffering was beyond description. We lost some to the cold and the blizzard and the frost. The Kurds had taken positions on two sides of the gorge. We managed to pierce through their lines. They popped up in front of you out of nowhere. They were afraid of neither the cold nor the blizzard. I lost in that gorge my beloved messenger Vahram of Chmshkatsag, whom I had sent on several occasions to Dersim and who had saved the lives of hundreds of Armenians.

"Our freedom was truly a miracle, we were surrounded in four directions. There were on the road hundreds of corpses, human and animal. We had to fight the enemy while clearing the road of the corpses so that the cannons and the carriages carrying the refugees could proceed. In the meantime we learned that the Turks had sent an army battalion via Fam to cut our lines. It was imperative to pass through that gorge and reach Karin where we could prepare for the great battle. Finally we managed to open a path and crossed the Chilek gorge.

"Prior to our retreat we destroyed all the depots of Erzincan and Mamakhatun. We had resolved with Colonel Moreli not to leave the Erzincan district, but what were we to do, fresh reinforcements did not arrive and we had to retreat. I always knew that with our present forces we could do no more. We waited for almost three months and fought as

Avetis Mushmulian (Awetis Chavush) of Kovtun. A volunteer from America, he participated in fourteen battles under Andranik, and decorated with the Georgian Cross. He was with Murad during the evacuation of Erzincan. He left for Cilicia in 1919, and was one of Epremian's cavalry. He was killed on August 15, 1920 in the battles of Chihun.

much as we could, always hoping that reinforcements were to arrive. Months passed and nobody came. I had wired them that if they failed to send fresh forces I would be calling them traitors to the fatherland."[101]

It was hard to hear those accusations from Murad, but there were some truth in them. As everywhere and at all times there is always next to the bravery and selflessness, individual those cases of collective desertions which history is regrettably obliged to record.

It is perhaps understandable that Murad and his comrades, isolated and deserted in one of the most dangerous areas of Turkish Armenia, would vent their rage on the party com-

Z. Keshishian of Shabin Karahisar

rades such as [Arshak] Jamalian who on the eve of the atrocities gave endless promises, all of which remained unfulfilled.

The bitterness also extended to Andranik who had been appointed the commander of the Armenian volunteer forces. Dragging his departure from the Caucasus, he arrived late at a time when the Turkish Armenian regions were endangered. He arrived only after the victorious Turkish and Kurdish hordes began looting and plundering in Erzurum.

Over fourteen years have passed since those tragic days. Now it will be possible to observe and comment on those events in a calm and collected manner.

Here is General Ghorghanian, who is perhaps one of our most fair-minded:

"Undoubtedly the signs of collapse became evident on the Caucasian front after the Bolshevik Revolution. Mass desertion occurred in every army unit, which then had to be replaced by Armenian ones that had been barely formed yet. The latter now had to shoulder the grave responsibility of defending with meager resources not only the huge front from Baberd to the Iranian Azerbaijan, but the fortresses such as those of Erzurum and Kars.

In the meantime it had to maintain and protect lines of communication and the railroad.

"On January 25, an official telegram stated not to hand over the defense of the Erzurum railway to the Armenians there. The Armenian forces occupying Turkish Armenia had to leave the country. It had become impossible to continue the fight anymore.

"Furthermore, the huge quantities of ammunitions left behind by the Russian forces had to be left in trustworthy hands.

"There was also the painful issue of the defense of the rear echelon. It was evident that the Tatar brigands under Turkish command were dismantling all important lines in the rear and making every effort to paralyze the Armenians who were already in an unequal struggle with the Turks: first the Baku-Tbilisi line, then Erevan-Julfa, and even the Tbilisi-Alexandropol line.

"In the meantime the Kurds had commenced their attacks on the Armenian villages, first in the province of Erevan, then in a number of mixed Armenian-Muslim regions. Numerous Armenian villages appealed to the national authorities and begged to be exempt from military service because their youth had to stay back and defend their families and fight against general anarchy.

"It was the main objective of the Turks, Kurds and Tatars to keep the Caucasian Armenians occupied with the defense of their hearths. Naturally the Russian Armenian soldiers fighting in Turkish Armenia were well aware of the danger to their families back home.

"It was under these conditions that Armenian contingents were asked to be sent to the Turkish Armenian front."[102]

Nevertheless, despite the highly unfavorable conditions in the Caucasus, many did leave for the front, many who had already gone to Turkish Armenia in the early days of the volunteer movement. Of course the enemy tried to stop them from coming back.

It also should not be forgotten that hundreds of Caucasian soldiers did not return from Turkey with their fleeing comrades. Despite the hopeless conditions at the front they stayed in dangerous positions such as Erzincan. They fought with glorious dedication along with Murad's legion against the common enemy and then helped in the retreat to the Caucasus.

Sepuh in his memoirs briefly described the excitement and enthusiasm of the Caucasian Armenian youth.

"...One day later the train was carrying a hundred and fifty Nersesian High School students to Erzurum to maintain the telephone lines. There were also a few doctors in the group. One had to be there to witness the spirit of these students heading to the front to serve their fatherland.

Of course many refused to go or fled the battlefields to save their skins. Nevertheless it is baseless and unfair to usurp the idea of a national entity and make judgments about the difference between Turkish Armenian and Russian Armenian youth. We are all of the same stock. We have always esteemed the Russian Armenian peasantry. From the early days of the movement thousands became martyrs in the land of Vaspurakan, Karin, and Taron.

However, the best among us, whether Russian Armenian or Turkish Armenian, have always been fewer than those who were indifferent, which is the case in every society. Our people too have an allegiance that is local like their brethren in Mush, Van, Sepastia, and so forth. Local allegiance always supercedes a collective one. During the Armeno-Tatar wars, our people of Varanda, Khachen, Ghapan willingly and whole-heartedly fought for the defense of their district, though they would never go with the same enthusiasm to fight in a given Russian Armenian district. Thus, moving from one place to another was for fierce characters like Nikol Duman.

In regard to this subject is a brief emotional talk between Murad and Chopur Davo, one of the Russian Armenian leaders, on the road to Mamakhatun. Here is Amirkhanian again:

"Chopur Davit, accompanied by Sargis Eazechian, who was later killed in the battle of Karakilise in May 1918, had arrived in Mamakhatun along with three hundred fighters and transport carriages.

"Murad, who loved Davo with whom he had gone through so much for so many years, said when he saw him, 'Treacherous criminals, you are the executors of two thousand innocent martyrs. I have no confidence in any of you anymore, you are all liars, you low-life.'

"Chopur Davit approached Murad with a jovial face, held his hand, and said, 'You have the right to be angry, Murad, my brother. Let me be sacrificed to your soul. Listen to me. None of the people you mention are real Armenians. They are alienated and estranged lads. I spit on their patriotism. I will talk to you about that later. Have all the boys on the Kghi front redeployed.'

"These words disarmed Murad. Coming to terms with Chopur, he immediately dispatched five horsemen to Kghi to inform the guards there. Then he ordered Chopur Davo to remain on the road to Erzurum with twenty soldiers."

Murad made several sharp and abrasive comments against a number of the Caucasian intellectuals. Many of these derogatory comments were addressed at poor old Aghamalian.[103]

Even Sepuh did not spare the poor old man.

It was said that he and his comrades embezzled thousands of rubles selling seventy-two cases of Mosin rifles and sixty thousand shells to the Turks.

The claim was that he and his lackeys said to those appealing for the refugees, "You are going to die and have no right to live because you cannot coexist with the Turks. The Turks are more educated and noble. You are guiltier than the Turks. Do not come to us. Go to your leaders."

It was also said that he had come into a secret agreement with the Turks to leave Karin to them in return for twenty thousand gold pieces, and so on and so forth. All this was written and published in a book in America, three years after the events, and no one dared to question the hot-blooded accusers.

I have not had the honor of knowing Aghamalian's so-called lackeys, but I knew him, so allow me to take this opportunity to defend this kind and innocent comrade.

I have known him since his adolescent years in Karabagh when along with many others, even before the establishment of the Dashnaktsutiwn, he had enrolled in the cause of the liberation of Turkish Armenia and was known for his puritan character and exemplary devotion. Christopher, who had a good instinct for knowing people, expressed his fascination for him. Tigran would continue to be remembered as such until the last days of his tragic martyrdom. It was for his high character that he had been appointed the plenipotentiary of the Union of Cities in Erzurum. I trust that he was not completely suitable for that position that is to say in regard to his practical abilities. He was not a practical man and was not called upon to be a leader during those stormy days in particular. But who among us would not assume responsibilities after the mass extermination of our intellectuals? Who among our activists has not been *Homme a tout faire* in the last fifteen years, be they a writer, publicist, preacher, organizer, public affairs leader, or even a diplomat?

Yet even Sepuh spoke against him.[104]

There was also talk about assassinating him. We heard of this in the very book published in Fresno: "A few brave Sepastian lads asked for Murad's permission to kill that despicable Aghamalian on the spot. Murad did not grant them permission and said that this would open doors to fratricides and dangerous developments.

It is an honor to Aghamalian and to the Armenian people that he was not killed by Armenians. After the fall of Kars, Aghamalian was executed by the order of the high Turkish commander. He entered his grave as a martyr to the national cause and not as a traitor of the fatherland.

* * *

But let us return to what followed the retreat.

Murad was now in Erzurum and there too the fighting forces were insufficient and the people in a pitiful condition. Andranik and his forces were still in Alexandropol but even his arrival would not save them. They had to be moved as soon as possible to Sarikamish.

Murad once again immersed himself in an impossible task. He and his comrades saw that they had to fend off Turkish attacks by strengthening the fortress town and maintain the railway and encourage the soldiers.

On February 20, 1917, when news arrived that Andranik had reached Hasan Kale, the joy was indescribable. But once again the Armenian people were over-enthusiastic and began to threaten the local Turkish population. Many even engaged in looting the Turkish neighborhoods and the latter, who were about twenty-five thousand in population, were in terror.

Murad was very concerned about this and meeting with the officers and their deputies demanded the utmost military discipline.

Our military capability was inferior to that of the enemy and there was really no hope of any assistance from the outside world. Even if Andranik were a Napoleon he would not be able to save and defend Erzurum nor Kars.

After a short and desperate resistance another retreat commenced, this time with Andranik at the helm.

They arrived in Kars. Shortly after the defense minister of Armenia, Mamikonian, also arrived, accompanied by a number of ministers. Sepuh and Murad did not receive a good reception there. The minister of defense himself admonished them, saying that the two prominent leaders were undisciplined and worked independently and even hurt the cause with their tactics.

According to Sepuh, these remarks pertained to the "cleansing" operations, which Murad had to carry out in the Turkish Armenian districts.

It seemed that he and other warriors had adopted a policy of an eye for an eye, like the one in the Caucasus during the Armeno-Tatar wars when our forces, outraged by the Tatar atrocities, were convinced that the an eye for an eye was the most effective way to restrain those blood-thirsty hordes and put a stop to the senseless battles,

Unfortunately this was part of our fate as well. Revenge would also echo in the halls of the western diplomatic circles upon whom our cause depended. We would not forget Lord Curzon's thunderous outrage against the Delegation from the Armenian Republic. It was in regard to the so-called "Armenian atrocities" while those of the enemy had to be tolerated, as if Europeans thought that Armenians were a superior race and should not have bloodied their hands with innocent women and children.

Nor is it surprising that Turkey's German ally reported "Armenian atrocities" in the news and voiced alarm from Constantinople to Berlin.

On May 3, 1918 the German Ambassador to Constantinople, Count Bernsdorf, formerly an ambassador to Washington, wired Berlin about Murad in the Erzincan district:

"In the district of Erzincan, during the Russian occupation 1916-1917, there were one thousand and five hundred Muslim residents. In general they commend the conduct of the occupation forces. But when the Russians departed Murad Pasha established a reign of terror.

"Six hundred Muslims from infants to the aged were killed. Hundreds disappeared. The city center turned into a pile of rubble and only the General Headquarters building remained standing."

The German Consul, [Franz] Andres reported the same to the Ministry of Foreign Affairs from Kars on May 16, 1918:

"On April 14 of this year, I departed Constantinople for Erzurum, my previous official station, and I crossed through many destroyed villages. When I stayed in Erzincan, which I had last seen in January 1914, it was unrecognizable. In December 1917, subsequent to the Turkish-Caucasian ceasefire, a reign of terror was led by Murad Pasha. Six hundred Muslims, from ages of three to seventy were killed. Hundred disappeared. During the March retreat, the Armenians made an attempt to destroy the building of the General Headquarters constructed by Zeki Pasha, but did not succeed."

After this period the two warriors, Murad and Sepuh, feeling offended and embittered, departed from the battlefront and went into temporary seclusion in Tbilisi.

Later, when the advance of the Turkish forces also threatened the capital of the Caucasus, they left Tbilisi as well.

Sepuh writes:

"We went to see some of the members of the National Bureau to ask for fifty horses and weapons so that we could head back to the front through the mountains. Unfortunately this proved futile. Left without weapons and horses we went by train, which was very difficult because the Turks of Borchalu stopped the cars and massacred anyone who looked suspicious.

"Having lost our hope with the National Council, we appealed to the Western Armenian Council. One of its prominent members was Vahan Papazian. He too replied that there was neither money nor weapons, but we were convinced there were and all that was lacking was leadership. Everybody was out of his mind. All we asked for was fifty thousand rubles and fifty rifles. Our objective was to purchase horses and go where Armenians were to meet their fate. Considering the situation the National Council rushed a delegation to Batum to come to an agreement with the Turks. All kinds of rumors began to circulate, for example that the Turks had occupied Akhaltskha and Akhalkalak and were about to enter Tbilisi in a few days via Borzhom. This was enough to create panic in the entire city. Anyone who could escape did. At the same time Hamo Baraghamian came to us and said the president of the National Council demanded that we leave Tbilisi or our lives would be in danger. But where were we supposed to go without weapons?"

* * *

It was painful for the old freedom fighters to have to leave the Caucasus. Sebouh writes in his memoirs "Murad then said, 'Why did not an enemy bullet pierce my heart and relieve this torture? You ask for a horse, they don't give you one. You ask for money, they refuse. And now the President of the National Council himself, our Great comrade Aharonian, asks us to leave the city. No, I am going to try again.'"

But his appeals were fruitless and they departed via the military path to the north. The first stop was Vladikavkaz and then Armavir, Tsaritsin, and Astrakhan. At each stop the Armenian communities embraced them.

This aimless wandering caused some among our ranks to call them "deserters." We have already mentioned who these types were.

Perhaps it was wrong for Murad and Sepuh to demand to serve independently when the commander-in-chief was General Nazarbekian. Andranik had made a similar demand. This is an issue that needs to be studied. Perhaps it was a sign of weakness. But let he who has gone through as much suffering cast the first stone at the hero of Kovtun.

There were also those who said that during the fighting from Erzurum to Kars. Murad and Sepuh secluded themselves and never participated, using their displeasure with Andranik as a pretext. Yes, their discontent and displeasure with Andranik was a fact, but it had deep and just roots, for it was true that it was extremely difficult to work with Andranik. Everybody knew this. But the accusation of their "seclusion" is absolutely baseless.

It is equally baseless to charge them with desertion, they who had been through the nightmare of such bloody events. Aharonian, the President of the National Council himself, refutes this in his memoirs:

"It was late March when we arrived in Sarikamish. The hills were still covered with snow. It was very cold. The forests were wrapped in the early morning fog. The soldiers had just woken up and were preparing the morning tea and getting warm. There was no sign of any complaint or despair. We witnessed the strong resolve of those unique boys. The towering element was again that marvelous Karabagh, and yet the main impression was of the unity among them, as if the entire Armenian nation was there to greet the enemy. This was the small army, which had for three months endured the fierce attacks from Sarikamish to Sardarabad to the deep gorges of Gugark–Karakilise.

"Our battalions were lined up without any confusion or fear. The infantry came out of the barracks armed and they lined up boldly on the slopes of the hills.

"'Murad and Sepuh!' said General Areshian, 'Hurry, get Murad and Sepuh to the front!'

"Barely half an hour passed before three hundred horsemen were following these gallant leaders and soaring toward the Turks, the cannon batteries lined up like a snake on the slopes of the hills.

"It was a fight for our Armenia."

* * *

Murad and Sepuh held meetings in Armavir. They consulted with the local committee and decided to go to Moscow. Russia was Bolshevik by now, and they wanted to have an audience with Lenin and ask for means to form an army and join the forces in Baku and then move westward and recapture the land that had become occupied by the Turks.

But it was difficult to open the way to Moscow. It was a turbulent period of civil wars. Rostov was still in the hands of Denikin. Murad and Sepuh moved to Tsaritsin through Armavir. There they contacted our comrades as well as the Bolshevik representatives. They learned that access to Moscow was impossible; the roads were too dangerous. They decided to appeal directly to Baku where fierce fights were being waged against the Turks. One of the founding fathers of the Dashnaktsutiwn, Rostom, was closely cooperating with Stepan Shahumian.

Murad and Sepuh dispatched two comrades to Baku for negotiations. As they were waiting for a reply they became acquainted with the Russian Bolshevik commander of Tsaritsin through some influential friends. Petrovski greeted the renowned Armenian comrades warmly and informed them that he had been appointed by Moscow as the commander of the Baku front. He added that he had a telegram order from Shahumian to provide the two warriors with money and weapons so that they could join those in Baku with their fighters.

At this moment the messenger who had been dispatched to Baku returned and confirmed Shahumian's order to Petrovski. On top of this they received a letter from Abraham Giwlkhandanian, who confirmed the decision in the name of the Dashnaktsutiwn in Baku.

The two hayduks took a ferry and headed in the direction of Astrakhan over the Volga River. They were in high spirits. New hopes were kindled in their souls. Turkish Armenia had been depopulated and the Caucasus was flooded with Turkish armies, but the cursed regime of the Tsars, that regime which had subjected the Armenians to so many evils and caused the depopulation of Turkish Armenia with its shameful retreats in 1915, was now toppled and Revolutionary Russia would expel the Turkish hordes from the Transcaucasus and create a united, free and independent Armenia. Lenin had already declared it so.

Poor Murad. What hopes he banked on this belief.

From Astrakhan he and Sepuh took a ferry and headed for Baku.

XIII

The Last Battle and Death

Following the battles of Sardarabad and Karakilise in June 1918, the Turkish military command concluded that it was incapable of crushing the Armenian resistance, and it was temporarily resigned from conquering Erevan and the country around Ararat. It shifted its forces toward Tatar Azerbaijan and their ethnic kin who had for months fought bloody battles to free themselves from the yoke of Russian Bolsheviks and expel the Armenians and Russians from their country.

On one side were the Armenian-Russian united forces of the Dashnaks, Bolsheviks, Mensheviks, and Social Revolutionaries, who wanted to defend Baku, the last front in the Transcaucasus of the pan-Russian revolution. On the other side were the Tatars and the Musavatist reactionaries. The leaders of the Russo-Armenian forces included Shahumian, General Bagratuni, Rostom, Abraham Giwlkhandanian and others. Lenin as governor of the entire Transcaucasus had appointed Shahumian, but his army alone was not enough to defend Baku.

The Tatars were filled with an irreconcilable hatred toward Armenians and they had already attempted to expel them in 1905. Our people knew that the Turkish army was coming to the help of its kinsmen and a Turco-Tatar victory would cause

Armenians grave consequences. Thus the Armenian Revolutionary Federation had decided to join the Russian Bolsheviks. Rostom and Shahumian, despite their deep ideological differences, worked hand in hand. On the other side the Georgian Menshevik government that was anti-Armenian cooperated with the reactionary Musavatist Tatars under the pretext of extinguishing the Bolshevik torch. They even dispatched auxiliary forces from Tbilisi and Turkish officers who began training the Tatars.

The German Military command had come up with a grand plan of turning Baku into an anchor for war operation against the British forces in Asia. It would mobilize the Muslim world and the Tatar masses in the Transcaucasus, Turkestan, Azerbaijan and Daghestan, as well as the Sarters, Circassians, Kyrgyzes, and so forth. Then it would march to Afghanistan and India and mobilize their Muslims against England.

This massive plan was aborted, thanks mainly to the Armenian partisans who fought against the Turco-Tatar forces from Baku to Geok Chai and from Shamakhi to Persian Azerbaijan.

But they fought, alas, without any thanks from some of those they helped. In the British House of Commons Ramsey McDonald asked what England was doing helping the Armenians. Prime Minister Balfour however responded. "His Majesty's government has a deep appreciation for their resistance and will do everything possible to get the necessary aid to them."

If the Armenian fighters put their weapons down, Baku would have probably fallen to the enemy before June of 1918. That would have been a major accomplishment for the German-Turkish forces. They would have been able to control the huge oil resources and head toward Turkestan, Persia, and Afghanistan, thus creating countless problems for the British armies in the Mesopotamia. The war would have been protracted and there might have been a delay to the Armistice in November 1918.

But Baku did not fall until September 17 of that year, thanks mainly to the Armenians.

Just as important for Armenians the battle of Baku had occupied the Turkish forces and thus greatly helped them in the Ararat region. It provided them a window of opportunity to recuperate from their long nightmare and to gain an opportunity to start building their free and independent republic.

And one of the major figures in the battle of Baku was our hero from Sepastia.

Rostom was right in saying to him and Sepuh when they arrived at the front: "The enemy is the same everywhere. If we defeat the enemy forces surrounding us, we will be weakening the forces threatening Armenia." The Turkish army was then moving in the direction of Baku under the command of Nuri Pasha.

Sepuh was in the battle and would thus be an eyewitness to what would happen to his heroic comrade.[104]

"Out there, in the distance, the cannons and rifles roared. Shahumian who had received us with open arms said, 'Can you hear the roar of those cannons? The enemy wants to conquer Baku, after which it will attack Erevan. To defend Baku is to defend the Republic. Go, rest, we will then provide you with all the resources you need so you can form your own Red Army.'"

"Moscow had responded to Shahumian's telegrams that it was not able to come to his help. The English could send reinforcements from Mesopotamia, and they in fact were already on their way, but the "Red Viceroy" Shahumian staunchly opposed the arrival of the English. Moscow, naturally, was against it as well.

"We appealed to him in the name of the Armenian people and asked him to see the situation with an open mind. We reminded him that if the Turks conquered Baku they would

Hamazasp [né Hamazasp Srvandztian]

advance toward the new Republic and put the entire Armenian population through the sword.

"Stepan Shahumian replied, 'I am aware of all that but I will do everything in my power not to let the English set foot in our country, even at the expense of Armenian blood. My decision is final. For me the entrance of the Turks in Baku is preferable to that of the English. When they move into a place they never leave.'"

Thus Baku was left to small contingents that were condemned to unavoidable losses. Out of contact with the rest of the world, deprived of the help of the Allied governments and lacking sufficient weapons and ammunitions, they weakened after almost eight months of bloody fighting. The small Armenian and Revolutionary forces could not hold against the surrounding Turkish armies, whose lines were reinforced on a daily basis by fresh contingents from Syria. In the meantime they had to fight against the Muslim mountaineers who rushed from the Daghestan heights to help their brethren.

Finally the English High Command dispatched some battalions from Mesopotamia, but they were not enough, and after seeing the strength of the enemy they deserted the battlefield and returned to the Caspian Sea toward Persia. The chaotic retreat of the English horrified the Armenians. They had banked their hopes on outside help. Desperation and desertion then overwhelmed them as well. The Turks were now bound to invade and the days of the city's survival were numbered.

Under siege Rostom, Murad, Sepuh and Abraham considered crossing the Caspian in armored barges and then reach the rear of the enemy. Shahumian approved the plan but they needed to consult with the other commanders such as Hamazasp[105] who was fighting near the Balajar station.

"When we woke the following morning," Sepuh writes in his memoirs, "Murad said, 'Last night I had a terrifying dream. I do not know what is going to happen. We, three of us were lying on the hill and were playing. Suddenly my musical instrument broke. I fell down from my position. I tried to stand up, but could not. Then I saw that my entire head was colored with coffee, including my fingernails and toes. The most surprising thing was that a mysterious hand came and colored the coffee in between my eyebrows. I tried to stand up and grab it but the spot where I was standing turned into a quicksand and then I suddenly woke up.'

"After the breakfast we took a car to the front with Stepan, Simon, and Grigor Ermenikiants, each of us in agreement with the plan. Murad said, 'I feel that something is going to happen today.'

General Dro (né Drastamat Kanaian)

"We sat in the automobile in silence.

"When we got to the tent Commander Sergo greeted us and then radioed Commander Hamazasp, who came quickly from the front riding on his beautiful steed.

"Hamazasp was pessimistic in regard to our forces. 'I suspect,' said the brave commander, 'that we can't defend Baku. Facing us is the formidable Nuri Pasha and our intelligence reports that he has just received a dispatch that he will be joined by fresh forces.'

"Just then a horseman came galloping from the Bibi Heyrat vicinity and told us our left flank was smashed and was retreating in the direction of the city and that the enemy would soon be entering Baku and cutting a path between our forces.

"Hamazasp rushed toward the front and ordered a reserve company to immediately depart for Ermenikend.

"Heading a group of fighters Murad and I also left for Ermenikend. Our appearance inspired the fighters with hope and courage, including those who were about to desert.

"But it would be Murad's last battle.

"The enemy machine guns began raining shells on our positions, but inspired by Murad's calls our fighters advanced while the enemy was retreating. After about three hours of fighting it was pushed back to the other side of the railway.

"It was a fierce battle, particularly on our left flank in the vicinity of Bibi Heyrat. The Turks had taken a hill and positioned their cannons and machine guns toward Bibi Heyrat.

"Murad said, 'We should also take positions but first we have to take the opposite hill.'

"I sensed the danger and said we should wait until Hamazasp's auxiliary forces arrived, but he insisted, 'If we wait the enemy can take the hill and we will not be able to hold our positions.'

"He lay down on the base of the hill. Stepan and I lay next to him. The Turks now concentrated their fire on the hill and tried to take it and cross to the rear of our fighters. It was a desperate battle on both sides. With the help of their machine guns, the Turks advanced and intensified their fire on our positions.

"Fresh Armenian fighters came to reinforce us, but their bravery could not silence the Turkish machine guns which continued incessantly and fiercely.

"Boys," shouted our hayduk for what would be his last time, "Let's open fire and silence those cursed guns.'

"Then came a scream and he was falling and rolling down the hill. A soldier leaped to catch his body, but he too fell vic-

Murad

tim to another shot and it became impossible to get them. It wasn't until two days later that we were able to reach them."

And it was there he would be buried, thousands of miles from his fatherland, there on the sand dunes of the Apsheron peninsula, there in the suburbs of the Tatar capital, under an alien sun, our gallant hero.

Suddenly the news of his death spread like a roar of the thunder. "Murad has been shot! Murad has been killed!"

With the ghosts of the massacres still hovering in the sky, the Caspian waves swept the shores as if in lamentation.

Did he sense the ruthless mockery of fate in his last seconds? Did he remember the long and bloody path that he had crossed? Did he recall Talvorik and the heights of Antioch? Did he remember his adolescent years when in the dark corners of Istanbul he carried out his first mission? Or the retreat from Erzincan to Kars or the blood-drenched body of his beloved Egho, the blizzard cold when he was paralyzed by typhoid and carried from cave to cave, the grinding of his teeth when he watched through binoculars his beloved family march with the caravan toward exile and their slaughter?

Rest in peace, comrade. Would that I had wings to fly over the horizon and kiss your lonely grave and cover it with roses I cannot. I am condemned to be away from your grave and those of Duman, Avo, Keri, Rostom, and Zawarian.

Your voice will continue from your grave to inspire our future generations. It will continue to encourage them to move on ceaselessly and fearlessly, always forward through difficult paths, struggling until that day when we will be free of our suffocating nightmare and take our place in the sun.

For our fatherland. For our freedom. For our honor.

Notes

1 Kovtun, Govdoon, at present Göydün in Turkey, one of the main villages in the upper plain of the Alis or Halis River, part of the Hafik District under the Ottoman Turkey administrative divisions. On the eve of the First World War, Kovtun, one of the nine entirely Armenian populated villages of the district, consisted of 300 households with a population of 3000. Prior to the 1915 Genocide and deportations of the Armenians, Kovtun had a population of 2,800 and 700 households. Between "1915–1924 there was no breathing souls living in the village." According to a visitor in 1979, the village was resettled by Turks and Circassians. The "Armenian school has been turned into a mosque and its destroyed church into a silo for storing barley. In 1915 the Turks razed and leveled to the ground Murad of Sepastia's native home." As recently as 1993, a group of tourists who visited Kovtun were amazed to learn that even to this day the elders of the village remembered the past history of Kovtun and Murad Pasha, and had ushered the visitors to a heap, which they identified as the site of Murad's house. For more on Kovtun consult V. Hambartsumian, *Village World: An Historical and Cultural Study of Govdoon*. Providence, RI, 2001. A. Ch'alapian, *Heghap'okhakan Demk'er* (Revolutionary Figures). Michigan, USA, 1991. For a detailed geographical, historical, and ethnographic history of Kovtun see A. Patrik, *Patmagirk' hushamatean Sebastioy ew gawari hayut'ean* (History-Memorial Book of Sepastia and its Armenian District). Volume 2. New Jersey, 1983, pp. 327–35.

2 Sepastia, Diospolis, Sivas, city and province, also known as Kabira founded in 150–100 B.C. Under the Ottomans, the city of Sepastia had a vibrant Armenian community of 30,000 with schools, cultural, religious, and social institutions. During the 1895–96 Hamidian massacres, over 1000 Armenians of the city lost their lives. The vast majority of the Armenian population of Sepastia was deported and sent by death marches to Der Zor desert and killed. Some of the survivors who managed to save their lives and escape to Armenia founded a new town, and named it in memory of their ancestral hometown Nor (New) Sepastia. For a comprehensive study of Sepastia, its fate during the 1915 Geno-

cide, and after, see Arakel Patrik, *Patmagirk' hushamatean Sebastioy ew gawari Hayut'ean*. New York, 1974–1983. S. M. Tsots'ikian, *Arewmtahay ashkharh* (Western Armenian Realm). New York, 1947, pp. 625–52. Haykazn G. Ghazarian, *Ts'eghaspan T'urkĕ* (The Genocidal Turk). Peyrut, 1968, pp. 86–118.

3 The reference is to Catholicos Mkrtich Khrimian (1820–1907), Prelate of Mush (1862), and Van (1880–1885), he served as the Patriarch of Constantinople for a brief period (1868). He was exiled by the Ottoman government to Jerusalem in 1890. Elected the Catholicos of All Armenians in 1892, he spent the rest of his life in Ejmiatsin. In 1878 he led the Armenian delegation to the Congress of Berlin. Catholicos Khrimian is recognized as the spiritual father of the Armenian liberation movement, and has left a rich legacy. For a comprehensive biographical study of Catholicos Khrimian see H. Achemian, *Hayots' Hayrik* (The Father of Armenians). Tavriz, 1929. Also consult, G. Giwzalian, *Khrimian Hayrik*. Beirut, 1954. E. Kostandyan, *Mkrtich Khrimyan, hasarakakan-kaghak'akan gortsuneut'yunĕ* (Mkrtich Khrimian: Social and Political Activities). Erevan, 2000. *Kristonya Hayastan Hanragitaran* (Christian Armenia Encyclopedia). Erevan, 2002, pp. 745–47.

4 Sepuh [né Arshak Nersesian] (1872–1940), freedom fighter, Armenian liberation movement leader, army commander. A member of the Hunchak Social Democratic Revolutionary Party, he joined the A.R.F. in 1892. He participated in a number of revolutionary operations, among them the Gum Gapu demonstration, followed by several resistance and self-defense battles, among them the Sasun uprising in 1894. He was one of the co-founders of the "One Child, One Gold" Foundation, through which with his comrad-in-arms, Murad, he managed to save numerous Armenian orphans. Sepuh participated in the fateful battle of Sardarapat, and later fought in Baku alongside Murad and others. After the sovietization of Armenia, Sepuh moved first to Constantinople, and later to the United States where he died in 1940.

5 Vardan Mamikonian (388/391–451), Armenian military commander who fought and fell in the epic battle of Avarayr against the Sasanid Persia in 451 A.D.

6 Daghestan, Dagestan, one of the 21 autonomous republics of the Russian Federation situated in the Northern Caucasus mountains. Daghestan is home to unusually ethnically diverse, and still largely tribal communities. The predominent majority of the Daghestanis are Sunni Muslims and speak various dialects of Turkish.

7 Tatar, derived from Ta-ta or Dada, a Mongolian tribe refers to the inhabitants of various regions and districts throughout Eastern Europe (Ukraine, Poland, Bulgaria, Romania), Russia, and Central Asia (Kaza-

khstan, Uzbekistan), also China, and Turkey. Before the 1917 Bolshevik Revolution, the name Tatar was used to designate numerous peoples from the Azeris in the Caucasus to tribes in Siberia. At present, Tatars live in the central and southern parts of Russia, with the heaviest concentration in Tatarstan, the Russian Federation. The number of the Tatars, predominantly Sunni Muslims, is estimated to exceed 10 million worldwide.

[8] Karin, Erzurum, city and district in Western Armenia, present day Turkey, on the banks of the Euphrates River. Because of its strategic location, the city has changed many hands during its history. Armenian community of Erzurum also suffered heavy casualties during the Hamidian massacres. The persecution of the Armenian community of Erzurum began in late January 1915 and reached its climax in July of the same year, when 19,000 strong Armenian community of Erzurum and its villagaes were deported to Derjan/Tercan/Erznka of which only 11 survived. The remnants of the Armenian communities were saved from the advancing Turkish army by a small contingent under the command of General Andranik and were relocated to Eastern Armenia.

[9] Erzincan, distorted for Erznka in Armenian, city on the right bank of the Euphrates River, the establishment of which can be traced to the eighth century B.C. The Armenian population of Erznka suffered heavy losses in 1895–96 massacres. In May 1915 the 15,000 strong Armenian community of Erznka was deported and almost entirely annihilated in the Kemakh Gorge. See Heinrich Vierbücher, *Armenia 1915*. Arlington, Massachusetts, 2006, pp. 47–51. Liberated for a brief period by the Russian armies in 1917, Erznka once again fell in the hands of the Turks after the latter's violation of the signed ceasefire. The remaining 4,000 Armenians of the district migrated with the retreating Armenian volunteer corps in the direction of the Caucasus.

[10] Kemakh, Kamakh, Kemah, Kamakhon, a fortress, village, fortress-town located in the Daranagh district of the Greater Armenia, near Erzincan, province of Erzurum, in present day Turkey, home to pre-Christian monuments of pagan Armenian gods. For more details see, *Hayastani ev harakits' shrjanneri teghanunneri bararan* (Dictionary of Toponymy of Armenia and Adjacent Territories), v. 2. Erevan, 1988, pp. 913–14.

[11] St. Karapet Monastery of Mush, Glakavank', Innaknian Vank, in the Taron district of Turuberan province of historic Greater Armenia near the city of Mush, was built by St. Gregory the Illuminator in early fourth century A.D. on the ruins of a pagan temple. In the nineteenth century, the monastery gained special prominence for having historic figures as its abbot such bishops as Mkrtich Khrimian, Garegin Srvandztian, and Maghakia Ormanian. In early 1900 it was the seat of a major diocese encompassing several major districts. Second to Ejmi-

atsin, it has been considered as the most important spiritual center in Armenia. Having survived the Genocide of the 1915 when it also served as place of refuge, it was completely destroyed in 1950 by the Turkish authorities.

[12] *Vardavar*, one of the five feasts of the Armenian Church related to the Transfiguration of Christ, a holiday with roots in pre-Christian Armenia.

[13] Andranik [Ozanian], (1865–1927) began his revolutionary activity in Sivas province in 1888. Joined the A.R.F. in 1892. He led guerrilla forces in Sasun from 1899 with 38 villages under his command and later assumed the leadersip of the Armenian communities of entire Bitlis and Mush districts. Disappointed and in disagreement with the orientation and policies of the A.R.F., General Andranik resigned from the party in 1907. After having spent some time in Geneva and Egypt, he identified himself with the Macedonian struggle where he led a troop of 230 Armenian volunteers in the First Balkan war (1912). In Transcaucasia after the outbreak of WWI, he commanded a volunteer troop of 1,000 men, on the North Persian front, contributing to the Russian victory at Diliman (Shahpur, April 1915). Later, his forces joined with the Armenian legion in expelling the Turks from south of Lake Van, but were forced to retreat by a Turkish counter-offensive (July 1915). Having resigned his command, Gen. Andranik left for Tbilisi in the same year, formed a new Western Armenian brigade, and did not participate in the fateful battle of Sardarabad. Discontented with the leaders of the Republic of Armenia for signing the treaty of Batum; recognized the government of Soviet Russia. He led his forces on Shushi (Karabagh) in December 1918, when a message from the British commander halted him, thereby causing Karabagh to remain outside Armenia to this day. To Ejmiatsin via Daralagiaz, March 1919; forced by British pressure to disband his brigade left Transcaucasia in April 1919; to Paris and London, trying to persuade Allies to occupy Turkish Armenia. He left for the USA to raise funds for the Armenian army. He died in 1927. General Andranik's body was planned to be sent for burial in Armenia. Refused entry by Communist authorities, his remains were laid to rest in Père Lachaise cemetery, Paris. By the wishes of Vazgen Manukian, the slain Primer Minister of the Republic of Armenia (1999), the remains of General Andranik were eventually transferred to Armenia and interred at a monument complex at the Erablur (Tri-Hill) Cemetery outside Yerevan. Several monuments in Armenia erected since independence commemorate the legacy of this legendary national hero and military commander.

[14] *Agha*, sir, master.

[15] Monastery of Hreshtakapet, the principal monastery of the Diocese of Sepastia and pilgrimage site for the Armenians of the Hafik district.

Located on the top of a mountain and fortified with walls it has been the summer residence of King Davit, son of the Armenian King Senekerim. A box discovered in 1871 is believed to have contained the remains of the Goharinian virgins. These relics were taken to the monastery and buried along the right walls of the church, in front of St. Hreshtakapet's painting. For more details see, Arakel N. Patrik, *Patmagirk'-Hushamatean Sebastioy ew gawari Hayut'ean*, vol. 1. New York, 1947, pp. 264–65. V. Hambardzumian, *Village World*. Providence, 2001, p. 41.

[16] *Lusnkay*, moonlight, moon-shine.

[17] "The dagger is your sacred weapon, the only hope of the world."

[18] Gum Gapu [Kum Kapu], a neighborhood in Constantinople where the Armenian Patriarchate is located. Here the reference is to the July 15, 1890 demonstration organized by the Armenian Social Democratic Hunchakian Party to bring the Armenian Question to the attention of the European representatives and to the implementation of the Article 61 of the Treaty of Berlin (1878).

[19] Hunchaks, refers to the members of the Hunchakian Social Democratic Party (HSDP), founded in 1887. On the history of the HSDP see A. Kitur, *Patmut'iwn S. D. Hnch'akean Kusakts'ut'ean, 1887–1962.* (History of S. D. Hunchakean Party 1887–1962), 2 vol. Peyrut', 1962–1963.

[20] The reference is to the reform Programs that were to be implemented in the Ottoman Empire to improve the condition of the Christian population.

[21] Babgen Siwni [né Petros Parian], (1879–1896), educated in Istanbul, joined the ranks of the A.R.F. He led the Ottoman Bank raid (August 1896) where he was killed early on in the siege.

[22] The reference is to Patriarch Matt'eos III Izmirlian of of the Patriarchate of Constantinople who served in two crucial terms: The Hamidian massacres of 1894–1896, and the Constitutional period in Turkey, 1908, and the Adana massacres of 1909.

[23] *Papakh*, lambskin high cap.

[24] *Fedayee*, freedom fighter.

[25] Armenian Revolutionary Federation [ARF] (Hay Heghap'okhakan Dashnakts'ut'iwn in Armenian), established in 1890 in Tbilisi, Georgia. For the genesis and evolution of the A.R.F. see M. Varandian's major study, *H. H. Dashnakts'ut'ean patmut'iwn* (History of the A. R. Federation). P'ariz, 1932.

[26] *Topa*, great.

[27] Bab-[i] Ali [Imperial Gate, High Gate, Sublime Porte], housed the divan, a relatively small council of ministers directed by the chief minister, the grand vizier. In the seventeenth century Bab-i Ali became the residence of the grand vizier of the Ottoman Empire.

[28] Kars, Ghars, historic fortress town in the Van district of the Ararat province of historic Greater Armenia situated in the present day Turkey on the border of neighboring Armenia. In the nineteenth century, Kars had a vibrant Armenian community and flourishing social, cultural, and religious institutions.

[29] Kristapor Mikayelian (1859–1905), one of the three founding members of the Armenian Revolutionary Federation. He was the editor of the Party official organ *Droshak* in Geneva, for a short period. He was killed in a bomb explosion on Mount Vitosh, Bulgaria, in 1905. For more on the life and legacy of K. Mikayelian, see A. Aharonean, *K'ristap'or Mik'ayelian*. Boston, 1926.

[30] The Storm, (*P'ot'orik* in Armenian) a movement formed by Kristapor Mikayelian in 1900, which extorted funds from wealthy Armenians to aid the national liberation movement.

[31] The Hamidian massacres, the reference is to the first major massacres of the Armenians under Sultan Abdul Hamid II during which over 200,000 Armenians were killed in a period of two years (1894–1896).

[32] The reference is to the massacre of the Protestants by the Catholics, which occurred in Paris on 24 August, 1572, and in the provinces of France in subsequent weeks.

[33] Aghbiwr Serob [né Serob Vardanian], (1864–1899), Armenian national liberation activist, freedom fighter. Having survived the Turkish government's persecutions, he escaped to Constantinople and later Romania. Upon his return to Western Armenia, Serop organized guerrilla cells in Bitlis, Khlat, and Sasun to fight against Turkish and Kurdish oppression, where he succeeded in saving many Armenian villages from definite death and plunder. Having earned the title of national hero, Serop was treacherously killed in the vicinity of the Geligözan village in Sasun along with his two brothers and son. His severed head was buried in the yard of the St. Karmrak church in Bitlis.

[34] Botsaris and Miaullis, prominent Greek patriots in the Greek War of Independence, who died fighting the Turks in the defense of Mesolóngion (1822–23) and at Karpenísion.

[35] "Avo is before my eyes and will remain forever. It was a summer day in 1906, when A. Aharonian and I in Tbilisi paid a visit to ailing Sepuh and other warriors of Sasun. They had temporarily taken residence at

Mantashov's *caravansaray*. Gathered around Sepuh's bed we were chatting, and while Murad, as usual, was joking and teased to boost the spirits of our comrades, another one caught our attention. One of the Sasun fighters, an unusual young lad, who never smiled and paced the room up and down quietly with a shiny dagger in his hand, which he constantly sharpened with an special fervor. He refrained from participating in our conversations. He did not even return our greetings, when we entered the room, nor did he even look at us. Head down, with his eyes gazed at his weapon with tiger-like movements he walked back and forth, constantly sharpening his weapon, examined his deadly weapon with a special attention like a parent who caressed his child. During our long stay there, we did not hear him utter a word nor a smile, not even a glance towards the guests or any interest in the conversations. He was immersed in his work or perhaps the visions of the impending fights.

He was Avo of Trebizond, spoke but little, shy, fast-paced and bold who competed with Murad in the Achillean exercises. He was an inseparable member of the Sepuh, Murad trinity. He was Avo the *Parmakhsz* (fingerless) one of greatest fighters unmatched in selflessness and devotion to the cause, whom ten years later, in the summer of 1916 we laid to rest in the Khojivank cemetery of Tbilisi next to [Nikol] Duman, Rosom [Zorian], Kei [Arshak Gafafian] and Simon Zawarian. *(V)*

[36] See *Hayrenik' Amsagir* (Hayrenik Monthly) 5, no. 5(53) (March 1927). *(V)*

[37] *Parmakhsz*, fingerless.

[38] *Kerotik*, medal, reward.

[39] Hayduk, hayduk, Hayduk, Heiduc, Heyduke and Heyduque, originally to have meant "robber" or "brigand," haidud in Turkish "marauder," hajdis (plural hajduk) in Hungarian/Magyar. In several Eastern European and Scandinavian countries, the term has also been referred to as the attendant in the court of law, male servant.

[40] *Vali*, governor of a province.

[41] *Droshak* (Flag), official organ of the A.R.F. founded in Tbilisi in 1891. After the release of its first two issues, it was moved to Geneva where it continued to published until 1914. Later a monthly (1925–1933), and between 1969–1985 a bi-weekly, *Droshak* was moved to Beirut, and then to Athens, Greece until the independence of Armenia in 1991 when shortly after, it was moved to Yerevan.

[42] Prince Alexey Borisovich Lobanov-Rostovsky (1824–1896), descendent of the Russian nobility, statesman, better known for having published the two volume set of the Russian Genealogical Book. He served

on various diplomatic capacities, such as ambassador, minister of foreign affairs, and played a major role in spreading Russian hegemony in the Balkans and in East Asia

43 *Pro Armenia*, French language bi-weekly established by Kristapor Mikayelian in France, 1900–1914 [from 1912–1913 under the title *Pour les peuples d'Orient*]. The main goal of the publication was to introduce the French and international community to the Armenian Question, raise awareness to the condition of the Armenians in the Ottoman Empire and provide information on the ongoing massacres and the Armenian liberation movement. It published reports, documents, and articles on the oppressive Turkish as well as Russification policies of the Tsarist Russia in the Caucasus. Its editorial board included a number of world-renowned French intellectuals, scholars and politicians.

44 Yildiz Kioshk (*Yıldız Kioşk* [Palace]) situated on the same-named hill comprises a group of buildings, which constitute an Ottoman Turkish Palace architecture. Sultan Ahmed I (1603–1617) built the first mansion of the complex on the land, which used to be a hunting ground of the sultans.

45 Armeno-Tatar War (1905–1906), refers to the clashes in the Transcaucasus between Armenians and Tatars, allegedly instigated by the Tsatrist Russian government, in which the A.R.F. took a predominant role in heading the Armenian community's self-defense activities, and radical measures to neutralize the destructive policies of the Tsarist government in the Transcaucasus, Armenia, in particular.

46 Zangezur, a region in the southern Armenia neighboring Iran, Azerbaijan and Nakhijevan.

47 *Haraj*, social, political, economic and literary daily. The official organ of the A.R.F. Eastern Bureau, later a publication of the A.R.F. Bureau in Yervan (1919–1920).

48 Avetis Aharonian (1866–1948) Armenian writer, politician and public figure. Upon completion of his elementary education and assuming various teaching positions in his native Igdir, Aharonian received his higher education in Lausanne and Paris, 1898–1901. He chaired the Armenian National Council, which proclaimed the independence of Armenia on May 28, 1918. As a member of parliament, he headed the Armenian delegation to the Paris Peace Conference, where he signed the Treaty of Sevres. Aharonian stayed on during negotiations leading to Treaty of Lausanne (July 1923), at which he protested. He settled in Marseilles. Paralyzed by a stroke while giving a speech in February 1934, Aharonian remained invalid for the rest of his life until his death in 1948.

[49] Ferdinand Foch, (1851–1929), member of the French General Staff, commandant of the Ecole de Guerre (War College). Army commander during the WWI, later Commander-in-Chief of the French Army. Upon conclusion of the War, Foch headed the Armistice negotiations and played a prominent role at the Paris Peace Conference.

[50] *Hayrenik' Amsagir* (Hayrenik Monthly) 6, no. 2(62) (December 1927). *(V)*

[51] Mihranian movement, named after a prominent A.R.F. *khmbapet* (group leader), refers to elements who gradually left the ranks of the A.R.F. and joined the Russian Social-Revolutionaries or Social-Democrats, forming Armenian sections within them in disagreement with the decisions adopted at the Third A.R.F. World Congress in regard to the "plan of action for the Caucasus." From 1904 to 1906, the eastern regions of the A.R.F. held consecutive *rayonakan* (regional) congresses. Their immediate concerns were the Armeno-Tatar confrontations, but the fundamental part of their agendas dealt with the participation of the peoples of the Caucasus in the Russian revolutionary movement, and the role of the A.R.F. in that movement. Some extreme leftist elements were nevertheless still dissatisfied. They did not wish to be concerned with the Turkish-Armenian cause and demanded a separation from the Russian-Armenian cause, intent on operating exclusively within the context of the Russian revolutionary movement. In turn, other elements—Western Armenian intellectuals, fieldworkers and fedayees, refused to accept this new phenomenon. Nor could they tolerate "socialism" and other socio-philosophical terms associated with it.

[52] "It was a true desecration . . . Those elements who with fake enthusiasm received and embraced the Commander of the Sasun fights with open arms. Today are oblivious to the memory of the hero [Andranik] to a degree that they do not even think of erecting a bust at his tomb, an act, which would require the least sacrifices on the part of our Paris bourgeosie. *(V)*

[53] Dashnaktsakan, Dashnakist, refers to the rank and file members of the A.R.F.

[54] Mikhayel T. Loris-Melikov, (1826–88), Russian general and statesman of Armenian descent. He was granted the title of the Count for his services in the Russo-Turkish War of 1877–78 and in 1880 was made minister of the interior by Tsar Alexander II. He is credited for promoting some liberal reforms, specifically in the educational system, which was presented and approved by Tsar Alexander II in 1884.

[55] *Hosannas*, an acclamation in welcoming a newcomer.

[56] You can find it in the A.R.F. archives. It is a long hand-written letter by Sepuh mailed form Gandzak to Geneva, where Andranik was at the

time and was in correspondence with his former company commanders and invited them to "Erkir" [Homeland] . . . Sasun. The Armeno-
Tatar clashes had subsided significantly and situations had calmed
down. *(V)*

57 Paruyr, *nom de guerre* of General Andranik.

58 See his article in *Hayrenik' Amsagir. (V)*

59 Named after Père François de la Chaise (1624–1709), a Jesuit cler-
gyman, the confessor of Louis XIV, it is one of the most famous ceme-
teries in the world. It is reputed to be the most visited cemetery in the
world, attracting hundreds of thousands of visitors a year to the graves
of those who have enhanced French life over the past 200 years. It is
also the location of five Great War memorials. Many prominent Armenian writers, intellectuals, political and and revolutionary characters are
also buried there.

60 Noted writer, Hayk Achemian in his major work titled *Hayots'
Hayrik* (Father of the Armenians) had visited that magnificent
monastery in 1925, located near the Turkish border in the present day
Western Azerbaijan province of Iran. For decades, it constituted one of
the major posts and places of refuge for our revolutionaries. Achemian
had recorded all the epigraphs of the monastery to release in one of his
future publications. *(V)*

61 In another place, Achemian says, "on the southern wall [of the
monastery] there is an inscription which recalls the names of
Andranik, Sepuh, Murad, Smbat of Mush and others. *(V)*

62 Abp. Nerses Melik-Tangian (1866–1948), one of the illustrious figures of the Armenian Church for the past century. Known for his
strong opposition and resistance to the confiscation of the Armenian
church property by the Tsarist Russia, he was appointed by Catholicos
Mkrtich Khrimian to a number of positions, among them, abbot of the
Monastery of Tatew', Prelate of Siwnik, Vaspurakan, Chancellor of the
Holy Ejmiatsin, and later as the Prelate of the Armenian Diocese of
Azerbaijan in Iran where he spent the rest of his life making major con-
tributions to its communities. Among many of his administrative, spiritual and social accomplishments, he is also hailed for his major
humanitarian efforts in saving the lives of thousands of Armenian and
Assyrian refugees who poured into Tabriz escaping Turkish atrocities in
the eastern provinces of the Ottoman Empire, Van in particular.

63 Monastery of Tat'ew, monastic complex in the Siwnik region of Armenia established in the IV century in the memory of Tat'eos, one of the
disciples of St. Thaddeus. It has been the Seat of the Diocese of Siwnik
since the VII century and a major spiritual and cultural center.

[64] *Qazi*, judge.

[65] *Bey*, notable gentleman, sir; also as title meaning Mr. as well as prince, ruler, chieftain, chief, head, master.

[66] Murad was an anti-socialist (so were some of our other leaders) without having any deeper understanding of the ideology of socialism. We have already recalled his fierce struggle against our so-called separatist socialists. Murad continued that struggle against two of our comrades, Eghishe Topchian and Avetis Shahkhatunian during the Fourth A.R.F. World Congress (Vienna, 1907). However, when the Assembly with the backing of Rostom and Zawarian issued a resolution in favor of socialism, and when Murad realized that Topchian and Shahkhatunian were both true patriots, who were ready to make the ultimate sacrifice for the Armenian people and the Armenian cause, when he realized that Kristapor Mikayelian, one of the progressive founders of the party is also is devoted to that universal ideology (not to confuse with Bolshevism)—at that point he complied with his comrades and joined the decision of the majority. *(V)*

[67] *Oba*, group of nomads under the rule of a chieftain, place where an oba, large tent, is encamped.

[68] In 1904, Andranik, Murad and other comrades were headed to the Monastery of St. Thaddeus in the Maku district from Vaspurakan, when Mesrop Avetisian of Maku was getting ready to depart for Vaspurakan with Vardan Shahbaz's group on military and logistical missions. *(V)*

[69] Garegin Nzhdeh [né G. Ter-Harutiunian], (1886–1957), a graduate of the military academy (1907) in Sofia, he joined the ranks of the A.R.F. in early adolescent years. He fought in Gen. Andranik's brigade in the 1912 Balkan War. Back in the Caucasus, Nzhdeh joined the Armenian volunteers, and later participated in the epic battles of Karakilise and Sardarapat in May 1918. One of the organizers of the first Armenian Republic's army after independence in 1918, Nzhdeh was appointed commander and was dispatched to Goghtan (Nakhichevan) in autumn 1919, and to Karabagh and Zangezur in 1920. After two years of resistance against the Bolshevik and Tatar forces (1920–1921) and the fall of the Armeinan republic, he left for Persia thence to Bulgaria. Invited by the A.R.F. Central Committee to the United States, in 1933, he established the A.R.F. youth organization (*Tseghakronner)*, later to be renamed as the Armenian Youth Federation of America. He left the U.S. for Germany, and later to Bulgaria where he was arrested in 1944 and sent to Siberia by the Russians where he died in exile.

[70] *Hürriyet*, literally, freedom in Turkish, refers to the fall of the autocratic regime of the Sultans in the Ottoman Empire in 1908 and the

establishment of the Constitutional regime and the accession to the power of the Young Turks.

[71] *Ittihadists*, refers to the members of the Committee of Union and Progress (CUP) or *Ittihad ve Terakki Cemiyeti*, the political party in power in the Ottoman Empire during the First World War, also known as the Young Turks.

[72] *Chartakhs,* a common form of dwelling used in Sepastia, Cilicia and elasewhere in Western Armenia. It also refers to a summer cottage or a small wooden house. It is also used contemptuously in reference to houses inhabited by the poor.

[73] *Leplepichi*, person who sells a Turkish snack made with chickpeas.

[74] *Azatamart*, social, political, literary weekly of the A.R.F. published in Constantinople (1910–1914).

[75] Barsegh Shahbaz was one of well trained, eloquent and promising youth, who in 1915, left his studies in law at the Paris University returned to Constantinople from where he was exiled alng with hundreds of our intellectuals and fell victim to the barbarities of the Ittihadists. *(V)*

[76] Armenak Mikayelian of Kovtun, at present in France. *(V)*

[77] The reference is to the Adana massacres in April 1909, which coincided with the counter-revolution staged by supporters of Sultan Abdul Hamid II (1876–1909) who had been forced to restore the Ottoman Constitution as a result of the 1908 Young Turk Revolution led by the Committee of Union and Progress (CUP). According to the reports, an estimated 4,437 Armenian dwellings were torched, resulting in the razing of nearly half the town, which some described the resulting inferno as a "holocaust." An estimated 30,000 Armenians were reported killed.

[78] The Sepastia Mother Cathedral. A massive and solid structure with a 300 feet high dome with only two such others, St. Stepanos in Smyrna and one in Erzurum. All three the works of the same architect. For many years, Bishops Petros Tahmizian and Torgom Gushakian, Shavarsh Vpt. Sahakian, and many others preached from its marble studded altar. Also, among others who spoke from the altar, include Shavarsh Vpt., Dr. Nazaret Taghawarian, Barsegh Shahbaz, and Murad. In winter 1915, the Turks removed the cross from the top of the dome, and in July of the same year, during the deportations and exile of the Sepastia Armenians, they dumped the church furniture's and fixtures and "sold" them to the Turkish public. Later, for a short while, the cathedral was turned into a Kemalist prison, a holy place that once was a place of worship for 300,000 Sepastia Armenians. Now, desecrated,

and its surrounding walls in half-ruins, it is used as the military depot. See Haykazn G. Ghazarian, *Ts'eghaspan T'urk'ĕ*. Peyrut, 1968.

[79] Let us remember Vardan Shahbaz, Bidza, Mkrtich of Zimar, and late Dr. Hayranian. *(V)*

[80] Murad is a great lad, not a thousand is worthy of him. He is worth a thousand.

[81] *Bashi-bozook*, [Turkish, bashi-bozuq], one in no special dress; *bashi*, headdress, and *bozuq*, disorderly, unkempt. A member of the Turkish irregulars, troops notorious in the nineteenth century for their brutality. *Webster's New Twentieth Century Dictionary of the English Language*, 2nd ed. New York, 1978, p. 154.

[82] Monastery of St. Nshan, the Seat of the Armenian Diocese of Sepastia, one of the most majestic and ancient monastic complexes of Western Armenia, the origins of which are traced back to St. Thaddeus. The treasury, library and fixtures of this millennia old monastery were looted and its structures gradually destroyed over the years. For details on the history of the monastery see H. Ghukas Inchichian. *Nor Hayastan*. H. Hamazasp Oskian, *Sepbastioy Vank'er?*. On the looting and destruction of the monastery see "Hayots' lk'eal goyk'eru ew kaluatsneru talane t'urk'eru koghme," in Haykazn G. Ghazarian, *Ts'eghaspan T'urk'ĕ*. Peyrut, 1968, pp. 226–41.

[83] Nicolai Hoff and Louis C. Westenenk, secretary-general of the Norwegian Ministry of War and Dutch colonial administrator, respectively, were appointed as inspectors-general for Eastern Anatolia on April 15, 1914 for the six vilayets of Turkey. Their mission was the culmination of a protracted and often fateful involvement of the Great Powers with the treatment of the Armenians within the Ottoman Empire, which was abandoned by the outbreak of the World War, marking the resolute end of the "Armenian Question".

[84] Turkish-Armenian *vilayets* (provinces) include Erzurum, Bitlis, Kharberd, Van, Trebizond, Kars, Tigranakert, Erzurum, Ardahan, Cilicia, Sepastia, and Yerevan.

[85] Mehmet Talât Pasha (1874–1921), the principal architect of the Armenian Genocide. Born in Edirne (Adrianople), he became active in the Young Turk movement seeking to overthrow Sultan Abdul Hamid. He joined the Committee of Union and Progress (CUP) and quickly emerged a leader in the secret organization.

After the 1908 Young Turk Revolution, Talaat became one of the most influential politicians of the Ottoman Empire. In 1909 he was appointed Minister of the Interior and then Minister of Posts. By 1912 he was Secretary General of the CUP, which in a year seized complete power in the Ottoman Empire.

[86] Pegasus, dedicated to Murad's horse was written by Poet Daniel Varuzhan. A close friend of Murad, Varuzhan was also the best man at his wedding.

[87] Sarikamish, strategic town on the border of the Ottoman Empire and Tsarist Russia during WWI, where over 25,000 Turkish soldiers lost their lives, fighting against the advancing Russian forces.

[88] *Khmbapet,* cell, group leader, company commander.

[89] This same Muammar, the massacrer of children, who a year later learned that Murad had arrived in Erzincan and was headed for Sepastia. Terrified he made preparations to escape to Caesarea. He died of tuberculosis with the thirst of Murad's blood in his heart.

[90] *Zulum*, injustice, oppression, tyranny.

[91] Zabel Esayian, (1878–1943), born in Scutari, a district of Constantinople, grew to become one of the exceptional Armenian woman writers of the twentieth century. A graduate of Sorbonne, she returned to her native Constantinople where she embarked on an active literary career. She was ranked with Krikor Zohrab, Siamanto, R. Zardarian, and Daniel Varuzhan. In 1927 she visited Soviet Armenia where she was invited to establish her permanent residence. Esayian left the comfortable Parisian life and moved to Armenia in 1933 with her children, where she taught courses in Comparative and French Literature. After coming to the defense of her colleagues Bakunts, Totovants, Armen and Mahari, Essayan was exiled in 1937 at the age of 55 where she is believed to have died in 1943.

[92] The segment of a song, which along with other memories, Mrs. Srbuhi [Murad's sister] remembers and keeps it with herself. *(V)*

[93] An old and veteran activist in Moscow through whose efforts, the Armenian Committee of Moscow was formed. A major organization mandated to contirbute to the rebirth of the Turkish Armenia. *(V)*

[94] *Hoja, Khoja* and "Mullah" all mean an 'imam.'

[95] *Muezzin*, (Turkish, *müezzin*), a servant at the mosque who leads the call to Friday service and the five daily prayers from one of the mosque's minarets.

[96] *Ulema, olama*, Muslim scholar specializing in Islamic studies.

[97] G. Korganoff [General Ghorghanian], *La Participation des Arméniéns a la Guerre Mondiale (1914–1918).*

[98] Ibid.

[99] *Mukhtar*, head of village, also used as a common surname.

[100] *Rayah*, a christian subject under an Ottoman ruler.

[101] Sepuh, *Ejer im Husheren* [Pages form My Memoir], volume 1. *(V)*

[102] Korganoff, *La Participation* . . . *(V)*

[103] He was the plenipotentiary representative of the Association of the Cities in Karin [Erzurum]. *(V)*

[104] Sepuh in the second volume of his book *Ejer im husheren* (Pages from My Memoirs) in the words of Murad unleashes accusations in the direction of the first Armenian prime minister, "our ex-comrade" [Hovhannes] Kajaznuni. Apparently, for the latter's alleged remark that during the darkest days of Kars, "we will sacrifice Kars, so that the Batum will be liberated." However, that was the aspiration and idea of the Georgian leaders, and Kajaznuni could have uttered those infamous words only sarcastically as a Georgian phrase. *(V)*

[105] Famous freedom fighter of Van, who in February 1921 was brutally killed in the Yerevan prison in the hands of the Armenian Bolsheviks.

Select Bibliography on Murad

Considering the rich legacy of Murad of Sepastia in the Armenian resistance and liberation movement, there must be more works on his life and legacy scattered in the Armenian sources, periodical press, and the primary sources, in particular, documents and reports in the A.R.F. and the Turkish government archives, and perhaps also those in Armenia. The list below presents a select number of works, which can serve as preliminary research material for future more extensive project on Murad of Sepastia.

Books

Andranik, Murat ew Poghos Nupar (Andranik, Murad and Poghos Nubar). K. Polis, 1920.

Esayian, Zabel. *Muradi chambordut'iwně* (Murad's Journey). Beirut, 1972.

_____. *How the Hero Mourad Journeyed form Sivas to Batum.* New York, [n. d.].

Hambardzumian, Vahan. *Giwghashkharh* (Village World). Paris, 1927.

_____. *Village World* [Giwghashkharh]: *An Historical Cultural Study of Govdoon.* Providence, RI, 2001. Translated by Murad A. Meneshian.

Hovannisian, Richard G., ed. *Armenian Sebastia/Sivas and Lesser Armenia.* Costa Mesa, 2004.

Contents: Richard G. Hovannisian, "Sebastia/Sivas," (1-44); Robert H. Hewsen, "Armenia on the Halys River: Lesser Armenia and Sebastia," (45-80); Ann Elizabeth Redgate, "Catholicos John III,s Against the Paulicians and the Paulicians of Tephrike," (81-110); S. Peter Cowe, "Armenian Immigration to the Sebastia Region, Tenth-Eleventh Centuries," (111-36); Souren E. Kolanjian, "Ukhtanes the Historian: Bishop of Edessa or of Sebastia?" (137-52); Christina Maranci, "Armenian Art and Architecture of Sebastia," (152-70); Bernard Coulie, "Armenian Manuscripts and Scriptoria of Sebastia," (171-206); Frank Andrew Stone, "Anatolia College and Sivas Teachers, College: Armenian Education in American Schools," (206-36); Barbara J. Merguerian, "The United States Consulate at Sivas, 1886-1908," (237-64); Barlow Der Mugrditchian, "A Farewell to the Armenians of Evdokia/Tokat," (265-304); Armin Kredian, "A Gurun Shawl on a Cairo Wall," (305-22); Murad A. Meneshian, "Rural Sebastia: The Village of Govdun," (323-56); Tamar M. Boyadjian and Rita Vorperian, "Vaoujan, Son of Sebastia," (357-72); Helen Sahagian, "Mary Louise Graffam, Ernest C. Partridge, and the Armenians of Sivas," (373-98); Simon Payaslian, "The Armenian Resistance at Shabin Karahisar, 1915," (399-426); Richard G. Hovannisian, "The Fate of Sebastia in the Aftermath of Genocide," (427-63).

Lazian, G. *Heghap'okhakan demk'er* (Revolutionary Figures). Gahire, 1954.

Malkhas. *Aprumner* (Reminiscences) vol. 1. Beirut, 1965.

Patrik, Arakel. *Patmagirk' hushamatean Sebastioy ew gawari hayut'ean* (History-Memorial Book of Sepastia and Armenians of the District). 2 v. New York, 1974–1983.

Varandian, Mikayel. *Murad*. Boston, 1931.

Articles and Chapters in Edited Works

Ch'alapian, Antranig. "Sebastats'i Murat," in *Heghap'okhakan demk'er* (Revolutionary Figures). Michigan, USA, 1991, pp. 309-70.

Editor. "Murati hushatetrĕ (Hunuar 1–Noyember 29, 1915)" (Murat's Diary: January 1 – November 29, 1915). *Vem* 1, no. 2 (November-December 1933): 122-27; 2, no. 3 (January-February): 98-108; 2, no. 4 (March–April): 94-108.

Gevorgyan, Hamlet. "Sebastats'i Murat," (Murad of Sepastia). *Garun* nos. 8-10 (1989): 33-36, 12-16, 57-64.

Giwlkhandanian, A. "Ogostos hingĕ (mi ej Bagui herosamartits')" (The Fifth of August: A Page from the Epic Battle of Baku), *Vem* 1, no. 2 (November–December 1933): 108-21.

Nersisian, Ashot. "Sebastats'i Murat (Murat Khrimian)," *Droshak* 28, no. 13 (July 13-26, 199): 27-31.

The following articles were published in a special, August 4, 1938 issue of the *Hayrenik' Daily* dedicated to the 20th death anniversary of Murad of Sepastia.

A. H. "Druag mĕ Murati Erznkayi keank'en," (An Episode from the Life of Murat in Erznka).

Arnak. "Mer ardi surberĕ," (Our Contemporary Saints).

Editorial. "Murati mahuan 20rd taredardzi art'iw," (On the Occasion of the 20th Death Anniversary of Murat).

Ejmiatsnets'i. "Hek'eat'ayin heros Muratĕ," (The Legendary Hero, Murat).

Ghazarian, Haykazn G. "Sebastats'i Murat," (Murat of Sepastia). Three part serial feature, August 4–6, 1938.

Gilean, A. A. "Arajin hay heghap'okhakanin handipums," My Encounter with the First Armenian Revolutionary).

Hakobian, Astur. "Kovtunts'i Murat," (Murat of Kovtun).

Hakobian, Hambardzum. "Murat ew Kovkasi jraghatsk'ĕ," (Murat and the Mills of the Caucasus).

Hambardzumian, A. "Murati demk'ĕ," (Murat's Face).

Martikian, Vahan. "Murat ew t'urk' hariwrapet Kiazimĕ," (Murat and the Turkish Captain Kiazim [Karabekir]).

Matoian, A. "K'ani mĕ husher Murati keank'en," (Few Memories from the Life of Murat).

Seferian, M. "Arajin handipums Muratin," (My First Encounter with Murat).

Sepuh, "Lachkani herosĕ," (Hero of Lachkan).

Ter Hovhannesian, Hovhannes. "Husher Muraten," (Memories of Murat).

Trdatian, T. "Gtser Murati hayreni gawari gortsuneut'enen," (Sketches from the Home District Activities of Murat).

Vahe, Armen. "Khohun razmikĕ," (The Thoughtful Warrior).